What people are

Naked in the Now

Naked in the Now presents a sensual, accessible, and playful guide for anyone committed to cultivating a nourishing spiritual life. Whether you're a beginner, a dabbler, or a seasoned practitioner, this is a manual brimming with practical insights to help you forge a deeper connection with your own true essence. Consider this book a trusted companion that you will refer to over and over again for profound and delightful meditations and rituals meant to heal and enrich your relationships with yourself, spirit, and the world.

Ari Honarvar, author of the critically acclaimed debut novel, *A Girl Called Rumi*, and founder of Dance for Freedom, a project garnering global support for Iranian protesters

Marijke is a beautiful writer who helps you create a more intimate relationship with the most valuable and worthy person in your life... you.

Susie Moore, bestselling author and top-rated podcast host of *Let It Be Easy*

If you have been interested in meditation but always found it too difficult—too time-consuming, and too boring, this book is for you. Marijke makes it as easy as (to use one of her own metaphors) slipping into a warm bubble bath. Then, once in, she gently guides you into the deeper waters of physical, psychological and spiritual practice, where you can begin to shed all the unwanted baggage that has prevented you from swimming in the now, naked and truly free!

Joel Morwood, Spiritual Director of The Center for Sacred Sciences, author of *The Way of Selflessness*

Reading *Naked in the Now* is like taking a masterclass on presence taught by a lifelong friend. Marijke's gentle encouragement and relatable stories teach a new approach to life, one with less suffering and more joy. Through its playful and seductive language, we are reminded of the lightness that exists when we get comfortable with our naked selves, stripped of the thoughts and beliefs that no longer serve us. This book is a must-read for anyone who finds themselves constantly wanting more but unsure where to find real satisfaction.

Sanni Honnold, life coach and cofounder of OutWild™, featured in *Free Solo*

A Fresh, Must-Read... *Naked in the Now* is for anyone that wants to accept a sacred and joyful invitation to play their way into the vibrant now. This book is much more than just a fresh take on meditation. Yes, it is lighthearted and fun, filled with creative, easy-to-understand exercises. But it is also deep in the most tantalizing of ways, with insightful new ways to view and practice age-old teachings. Without even trying, you will find your pain has been eased and you have a smile on your face. *Naked in the Now* will skillfully awaken a divine place in your soul that might just be dormant. And on the other side is a sense of aliveness—as if the silence and the space all around you have become lit up from within.

Marni Freedman, author *Permission to Roar*, co-founder San Diego Writers Festival

Intimate, inspiring, and beautifully written, *Naked in the Now* is the ultimate guide to romancing your own soul. Embrace this book like you would your most sacred lover, for it delves deep into the essence of how to come back to ourselves, in fresh and exciting ways. It is a treasure trove of wisdom and heart with insights and practices to enliven and awaken us all!

Cherie Kephart, award-winning author of *A Few Minor Adjustments*

I strongly recommend reading *Naked in the Now: Juicy Practices for Getting Present* if you feel drawn to find your real, authentic self and want to find joy living in the moment.
Nere Lartitegui PhD, author of *The Missing Peace*

Naked in the Now takes the reader on a journey to bring more confidence and awareness to their mind, body, and spirit. Marijke naturally blends relatable lessons from her own lived experiences with supportive tools to help the reader tap into their own personal transformation and the transformation of their relationships. The exercises are meticulously designed to help the reader explore themselves on different levels and vary from easy-to-follow breathing exercises with big impacts to more introspective practices that you'll find yourselves revisiting time and time again.
Courtney Sanford, event producer and community builder, cofounder OutWild™

In reading this book, I am reminded to stay present at many levels. I love the manner in which Marijke shares her own journey as part of the process of helping the reader to be right there with her in the discovery of how to make the new connection to spirituality in the present moment.
Paul Steinkoenig, psychotherapist, former National Capital Area Disaster Relief assistant director for American Red Cross, sculptor

My drag is my personal practice of self-love, acceptance and expression — it's my playground where anything is possible. I see the practices Marijke offers with her inner striptease doing the same thing. Her practices encourage us to discard old conditioning and reveal our wild and authentic inner selves. Either way, it's about getting naked in the now!
Pattie Gonia, drag queen, environmental and LGBTQ+ activist, and community organizer

Previous Books

More ... Journey to Mystical Union through the Sacred and the Profane, written under pen name Mariah McKenzie

Publisher: O-Books (June 24, 2016)
ISBN-10: 1785352628
ISBN-13: 978-1785352621

Printed and bound by CPI Group (UK) Ltd, Croydon, CR0 4YY

For Rudra
"One, not two."

Naked in the Now

Juicy Practices for Getting Present

Naked in the Now

Juicy Practices for Getting Present

By Marijke McCandless

BOOKS

Winchester, UK
Washington, USA

CollectiveInk

First published by O-Books, 2024
O-Books is an imprint of Collective Ink Ltd.,
Unit 11, Shepperton House, 89 Shepperton Road, London, N1 3DF
office@collectiveinkbooks.com
www.collectiveinkbooks.com
www.o-books.com

For distributor details and how to order please visit the 'Ordering' section on our website.

Text copyright: Marijke McCandless 2023

ISBN: 978 1 80341 567 3
978 1 80341 574 1 (ebook)
Library of Congress Control Number: 2023937334

A CIP catalogue record for this book is available from the British Library.

Design: Lapiz Digital Services

UK: Printed and bound by CPI Group (UK) Ltd, Croydon, CR0 4YY
Printed in North America by CPI GPS partners

Portions of Chapter 4 reference Cheri Huber's work, including her "recording and listening" practice, reprinted by permission of Living Compassion (Cheri Huber).
Portions of Chapter 8 reference Julian Treasure's Ted Talk "5 Ways to Listen Better," reprinted by permission of Julian Treasure, with his name and link to his website; and Sanni Honnold's "Effective Communication: How to Have a Hard Conversation" workshop, reprinted by permission of Sanni Honnold.

The author of this book does not dispense medical advice or prescribe the use of any technique as a form of treatment for physical, emotional, or medical problems without the advice of a physician, either directly or indirectly. The intent of the author is only to offer information of a general nature to help you in your quest for emotional and spiritual well-being. In the event you use any of the information in this book for yourself, which is your constitutional right, the author and the publisher assume no responsibility for your actions.

We operate a distinctive and ethical publishing philosophy in all areas of our business, from our global network of authors to production and worldwide distribution.

Contents

Dear Reader,

Do you yearn for more juiciness, playfulness, and vitality in your life?

Have you heard about the benefits of "being present" but aren't entirely sure what that means or how to experience it yourself?

Would you like to be encouraged and supported in developing a sustainable awareness and self-inquiry practice?

What if being present were as freeing as being seduced by a lover?

Over the last twenty-five years, these questions have driven me to become a seeker and awareness practitioner, meditate daily, remember the magic of playfulness, examine my thoughts while diving headlong into my messy life, and find time to be quiet and reboot.

Learning how to find my own answers to these questions is what propels me to want to share with you my journey of discovery so that you can embark on your own.

I have traveled this road before. I have fought the demons of PTSD whose voices scream that I must stay on high alert all the time, saying it's not safe to relax. I have listened to voices telling me the only way to get things done is through righteous anger. I have cowered under berating voices saying, "I am inadequate, not enough." So, I know what it feels like to long for sweet intimacy, not only with my partner, but with Life itself.

I have felt the deep longing in my soul for something more—a yearning that seems to occur alongside voices in the head saying, "I don't want to. I don't feel like it."

I also know what it feels like to be driven by the desire for perfection. I am accustomed to striving for success. I was a straight-A student. I rose through the corporate ranks to the VP level; I started several of my own businesses and have a strong and capable mind.

But the constant striving for perfection had a downside. I judged myself (and others) for failing to be perfect—for not being competent 100 percent of the time, not being wildly successful 100 percent of the time, and not being unconditionally loving 100 percent of the time. I saw the world and myself as broken because we were not perfect.

I learned firsthand I had to relax and accept myself exactly as I was before I could end my suffering. I had to befriend my crying-every-day-for-seven-years self. I had to find juicy "okayness" right now. And by that, I don't mean uttering platitudes to myself. I mean owning that I am inherently imperfect—and yet wholly lovable.

Today, I practice delighting in life as it is. I willingly adopt a playful attitude because it decreases suffering. I notice my thoughts while meditating, recognizing that they come and go, no longer berating myself for having them but not being consumed by them. I think of this as learning to befriend myself.

And, I am free to befriend you too. I will accept you as you are and help you become however you want to be.

Imagine, if you will, this journey of self-discovery is like hiking a new trail that winds its way through a wild, somewhat forbidding forest, to an unseen peak. Would you feel better if you had a friend along? Would you feel even better if that friend had traveled down that trail before and could point out the dens of wild animals and the vistas along the way?

Let me be your friend on this journey of self-discovery. As you begin to strip away what no longer serves, let me introduce you to new concepts and a new vocabulary so you can explore them more fully. Let me hold your hand when negative voices in your head begin to criticize. I know what that's like. I've been there. I remember when I thought "worry," for instance, was real and that I was actually helping solve the problem by worrying.

Let me help you find a sweet path forward while we scale the cliffs of consciousness, daring to enter the unknown.

In the pages that follow we'll break through your fears of intimacy to discover the shocking juiciness of being naked in the now. Be prepared for an exhilarating and let-your-hair-down guide that will lead you back to the self-love you desire. Come join me as we develop an awareness practice that encourages more intimacy with ourselves, our loved ones, and Life itself so that we can rest easy, naked in the now.

With love,
Marijke (aka Prema)

Acknowledgments

In Gratitude

I first thought about writing this book in 2018. I took notes, met with my coach, Marni Freedman, and wrote about 18 pages. Thank you to *Alpine Writers Guild*, especially Marla, Catherine, and David, for reading this early draft. It became clear that the words were not yet flowing and the tone needed to be adjusted.

I put it down for two years. In those two years, a lot happened. First, I continued going on silent retreats for 20 days each year. Those retreats gave me the space to rest in a more profound truth and helped me forge some essential practices in this book. Second, I realized that I needed to correct my outward identity. I had chosen to write my memoir, *More … Journey to Mystical Union Through the Sacred and the Profane*, under a pen name. I felt good about the decision, but later when I went to write this book, I realized that my identity was confused.

In 2020, just as Covid hit, I embarked on a rebranding campaign. In July, I launched my new website and allowed my pen name's identity to be associated with me. I also began working on this book again. Thank you Jeniffer and Chad Thompson of Monkey C. Media for the fantastic job, helping me rebrand and put together a new website. I still love it.

Shortly after the website launch, I was ready to dive back into writing this book and was fortunate to join Marni's *Friday Readers Read & Critique Group*. The beautiful writers of this group: Marni, Lindsay, Janet, Caroline, Heather, Nere, Lenore, Nancy, Paul, Susan, and Valerie, were invaluable in helping me find the right tone and letting me know when I missed the mark.

In 2021, I decided to stop writing the book and instead took on the daunting task of writing a proposal. I want to give a shout-out to some agents who didn't take me on but offered me free and invaluable advice. Thank you, Lisa Hagan, for answering numerous emails, and thank you, Wendy Keller, for your relentless insistence on the importance of developing a platform!

At the end of the year, I finished the book, sent it to beta readers, and, after incorporating their suggestions, had it copyedited. Thank you to the beta readers who offered me valuable insights. Durga, my first meditation teacher and now dearest friend, was the first reader I dared share it with, and I appreciated her commentary about the chapters that worked for her. Jackie (a participant of my *Write Now Mind community*) was thorough, thoughtful, honest, and helpful in answering all my "questions for beta readers." I appreciated the time and attention she took in noting which sections drew her in and which didn't. Her feedback was instrumental in a few key decisions. Dilia provided a gorgeous rewording of a critical sentence at the very start, an overview of her takeaways, and brilliant marketing advice. Marla offered her valued opinion on the overall flow of the writing, as well as insights for making exercises accessible and relevant to all.

Thanks to my beloved copy editor, Shirley Clukey (who also copyedited *More*), for working with the first 50 pages. Shirley contracted long Covid and could not complete the rest of the manuscript, but reaching out to her was an essential step for me. A big thank you to Sarah Thwaite for her excellent job copyediting the rest of the manuscript. (And thank you to Brenda Copeland for referring me to her!)

Around this time, I also began reaching out to people for endorsements. Reaching out is scary! I want to hug Susie Moore for being a fantastic human who litters the world with contagious, encouraging energy, and a big thank you for offering a gorgeous (and my first) *Naked in the Now* blurb. It was a turning point for me to receive her endorsement. I could see the book on the shelves after that. Others stepped up, too, and with each one, I felt supported and encouraged to keep going. Thank you, Marni Freedman, Susan Keith, Paul Steinkoenig, Sanni Honnold, Courtney Sanford, Cheri Kephart, Nere Lartitegui, and Joel Morwood. As Joel has been a beloved spiritual mentor since 2009, receiving his words was especially sweet. His guidance changed my life. Thank you, Ari Honarvar and Pattie Gonia, who I pestered in the middle of crazy busy times for them, and who offered me their support and encouragement anyway.

Along the way, while writing this book, I thrived from the vulnerability and compassion of the *Write Now Mind* community. When getting vulnerable, it helps to see others willing to be vulnerable too.

I want to talk about what was different in writing this book from the last one I wrote under a pen name. Although I felt good about my prior decision to insulate my family by writing under a pen name, it was also excruciating to keep a secret. There were tough times when I could have used a hug, and celebratory times when I missed being able to tell them. This time was different. My family was there, and I felt so much love, support, and encouragement in writing this, especially from my kids and their husbands.

Thank you, Jaime, Jason, Sanni, and Alex, for being there for me through all the ups and downs of the last year in writing this book! It has meant everything to me to share this with you.

Thank you Collective Ink, my publisher, and the wonderful people with whom I have worked, especially GL Davies for seeing the potential, and Frank Smecker for holding my hand so kindly through the manuscript prep and final copyediting phase.

Finally, as always, a deep bow to my beloved husband, Jay (whom I call Rudra). Rudra has provided financial (and emotional) support during this process, for which I am grateful. Rudra is also my orienting compass. He knows my deepest heart's desire and tells me when I go astray. Writing this book and getting it out there is important to me, but not at the expense of living by the principles I share. Rudra reminds me to live Naked in the Now—every day. With Rudra, I am encouraged to stay humble, to keep my highest aspiration to spread unconditional love, front and center, and to remember our deepest shared truth: "One, not two."

Introduction

Oh! How can I be here and now, that naked, that open?
—Adyashanti

It is living in the naked now, the "sacrament of the moment," that will teach us how to actually experience our experiences, whether good, bad or ugly, and how to let them transform us.
—Richard Rohr

Over the years, I've come to appreciate the power of being naked. And yes, I use that term consciously to invoke the typical conditioned response to being naked: vulnerability, exposure, judgment, shame, and fear, but also to point to the juiciness connected to nakedness: innocence, playfulness, intimacy, passion, and love.

I invite you to let go of the former and welcome the latter, to explore for yourself life without the coverings of thoughts *about* life, to feel what it is to be truly present. To experience what I call "naked awareness."

Being naked in the now means dropping pretenses, thoughts, tensions, pressures, and desires. In our minds, we often rehash stories that happened in the past, or invent stories about what might happen in the future. These stories draw our attention away from the present. To get naked in the now, we must practice turning our attention away from what's going on in our head and redirecting it to the present moment. One way is by tuning in to what I think of as the sensual now (our physical reality), noticing what we see, hear, sense, taste, and/or smell. I like to think of it as getting intimate with the moment. This one. Right now.

Embarking on the practice of being present in the moment is no small feat. It requires us to accept ourselves as we are,

1

not judging ourselves or fearing being judged by others, and not, for a moment, striving to improve. This is not easy. Our conditioning thwarts us relentlessly. In our culture nakedness has become a ripe arena for judgment and shame. We don't dare expose ourselves for fear of ridicule and contempt.

It may seem like I am only talking about psychological nakedness, and for the most part I am, but consider the impact of how we, as a society, deal with physical nakedness, too. Society at large simultaneously shuns physical nakedness and secretly supports it... but only if we look a certain way, presumably like those on magazine covers.

This fear of being naked in any form presents itself in archetypal dreams where we are appalled to find ourselves physically naked in public. Being accidentally naked in front of others seems terrifying. We run around searching for clothes in our naked stress dreams, and we run around in real life covering up our authentic expression, not wanting to appear weak, not wanting to be rejected, seeking only to be presentable in the eyes of society.

I want to interrupt this conditioning and encourage us all to learn how to rest at ease in the moment as it is, with ourselves as we are, naked and open.

Within these pages, you will discover a different perspective—a spiritual one—that reminds us of the juiciness of life available now. Here is your invitation to get naked without fear, and redefine what being "presentable" means, through a collection of techniques, tools, and playful practices—all of which support a different worldview, one that

- honors being present over constant action,
- rewards mindfulness rather than judgment, and
- sees nakedness as beautiful and celebrated rather than shameful or weak.

Being naked in the now is a powerful and seductive opening to something different, something more. Mystics over the ages have repeatedly pointed to the same discovery: life exists Now. They have pointed to our capacity for direct experience of naked awareness for hundreds if not thousands of years. Modern-day spiritual teachers make the same claim. This book draws upon the wisdom of several living sages, including Eckhart Tolle, Byron Katie, Adyashanti, Cheri Huber, Joel Morwood, Richard Rohr, and more—all of whom teach of the potential richness of living "naked in the now."

For me, discovering this juicy potential meant a lot of different things. It meant learning to stabilize my attention through meditation; it meant being willing to listen without judgment; it meant being willing to expose deep, shameful secrets; it meant learning how to be physically intimate in a new way; it meant investigating my own thoughts and rooting out those which caused suffering; but mostly it meant learning to rest naked in the now both by myself and with my beloved every day.

Within these pages, you'll be introduced to practices you can do alone, plus a few you can do with others. Both can help you gain understanding of your own being. Both can uncover thoughts that keep you from being present. In Chapter 3, you will learn how to relax and rest, before tuning in to your own inner guide in Chapter 4. Chapter 5 brings you practices for getting to know yourself, including your pesky thoughts. In Chapter 6, you'll partake in an inner striptease where you'll discover your own naked being. Then, in Chapters 7, 8, and 9, you will learn how to rejuvenate and restore important relationships in your life, including how to evoke the power of presence. Chapter 10 has you exploring practices that encourage you to get psychologically vulnerable with another, while Chapter 11 introduces some playful practices to build relationships with friends or a partner. Finally, in Chapter 12, you will be invited to dive even deeper to bridge both psychological and physical intimacy, touching and being with another in the spirit of holy intimacy, while in Chapter 13 you will be invited to take yourself on a retreat filled with holy leisure.

You won't regret learning to "skinny dip" in the moment.

Chapter 1

Seeking Satisfaction

I can't get no satisfaction.
— The Rolling Stones

A few years ago, as I sat in a circle with other awareness practitioners, our teacher asked us, "Why are you here?"

The question generated some lively discussion about escaping from the rat race, but eventually we settled down to look at the question from a deeper perspective. Someone said we are here because of Dukkha.

Dukkha? What is Dukkha?

The teacher answered the unspoken question.

"Dukkha is a Sanskrit word most commonly translated to mean 'suffering.' Buddhists say that everyone suffers."

We pondered the concept of Dukkha quietly for a bit. Then a woman raised her hand.

"But I am not really suffering like that," she offered. "I am a mother of two wonderful children, in a happy marriage, with a job I like, and I haven't really had any horrible traumas happen to me... it's just that..."

She trailed off, then took a deep breath and started again.

"Before coming out to this retreat my little boy asked me a question. He asked if I was going away because I was sad. I quickly told him, 'No, I'm not sad. I'm happy being your mommy!'

"He sat for a minute, then asked, 'Mommy, are you going to "settle your body"?'

"Settling the body," she explained to us, "is a new term that modern parents use to encourage kids to get centered when

5

they are having a tantrum. These days we don't put our kids into time-out; instead, we gently encourage them to tune into their body and to intentionally settle the body down.

"When he mentioned that to me, I saw immediately he was right. That's what I need. I need to settle my body. I feel... unsettled."

"Yes," the teacher said, nodding. "Dukkha is most often translated as suffering, but it does not only mean some kind of intense anguish or horrible life circumstances—it also means a kind of persistent dissatisfaction—a constant restlessness that something is wrong and could be better or different. It's a feeling that contributes to tension perpetually held in the body."

"Oh!" A look of recognition passed over the mother's face. "Yes. Yes—that's it. I feel a nagging undercurrent of dissatisfaction almost always, which seems to build up, leaving me more and more tense and ill at ease with my life, despite the outwardly positive circumstances."

So, I ask, why are *you* here?

Why are you holding this book right now, reading these words?

The fundamental question of "Why am I here?" is worth coming back to time and again. It can clarify what you aspire to, what you hope for, what your priorities are, what you value.

Often it points to a feeling that something is amiss.

Like this mother, you may have followed a prescription that society sets forth, such as the American Dream, as the path to happiness, but come up feeling less than satisfied, restless maybe, or perhaps as if something is wrong with you or with the world, leaving you wondering, "Is this all there is?"

We are conditioned beings who often feel a persistent sense of dissatisfaction, of something missing, of not enough. We long to get out of the mind view that something is perpetually wrong with life—to discover for ourselves that nothing is ever "wrong" in the Now.

Maybe you've felt a nagging sense of—not really unhappiness, but not happiness either—what my husband, Jay, called a splinter in his being.

Or maybe, like me, you've experienced a crushing life crisis, such as your life partner cheating on you or childhood sexual trauma—events that can bring everything you thought you knew about life crashing down around you.

So, how to interrupt that tendency of the mind to scour for all that is wrong and missing? How do we rest at ease in the moment when so much is calling for our attention to be "fixed"?

The short answer is, we directly experience ease for ourselves.

Everyone can taste what it's like to settle down and rest at ease in the present moment. And a taste is all that's really needed. One favorite teacher of mine, Adyashanti, says all you need is *five seconds* of pure awareness to interrupt the persistent harping on something wrong, something needing to be fixed. Once tasted, it is natural to follow the thread—to dis-identify with perpetual dissatisfaction, to stop believing the negative voices in your head saying you are not enough—that life is broken.

Trauma and the sense of something wrong or missing became the impetus for both my husband and me to start a lifelong journey of self-examination and awareness practice. The journey led me to question everything I thought I knew to be true and to discover for myself the source of my own abiding happiness.

If we are not that nagging, persistent voice of dissatisfaction, then what are we?

Are we our thoughts? Our desires?

Are we our body? Our mind?

Are we the accumulation of what we do? The things we own?

Are we our values? Our morals?

Are we the sum of the things we did well, minus the things we didn't do well?

Rather than attempting to answer these questions, try this quick experiment. Take a moment, right now, and remember yourself as a child.

There you were, engaged in child activities in a child's body, with a child's mind... simply aware. Check in right *now* to that sense of simple awareness, that deep-seated knowing that you exist and that you are aware. Do you have the sense, even though you don't typically think of it this way, that, like a child, you are patiently and curiously watching everything as it seamlessly unfolds? Can you sense the same underlying awareness as your child self, even though your current circumstances are radically different? In every moment, regardless of the particular circumstances—our age or health, our self-assessed brilliance or stupidity—that same awareness persists, unchanged and available.

And what *is* it?

It is *judgment-free,* ever-present, unwavering, "is-ness." It is your naked being. It is who you are.

What would life be like if there were never anything wrong? Never anything to fix? Not that we wouldn't still follow what moves us, but that we wouldn't judge our lives by the outcome. We wouldn't need life to go a certain way *in order* to be happy.

Despite any supposed certainty about what we need in order to be happy—a new car, a new president, more money, world peace—none of those things are actually needed to rest in ease. The only real need is to touch who you are at the core of your being—to be present *now*, and rest there.

In fact, we often experience this still, full, naked being. It's just that in our conditioned striving for perfection, we overlook it. We catch it sometimes, though, in certain kinds of moments, like in a moment of delight when a butterfly alights on our hand, or during the love and stillness present during passionate sex. We might get a glimpse in the moment when our best friend laughs and hugs us in silly, lighthearted playfulness. But we also see it in times of trouble, when all our well-laid plans are thrown out the window because we have just learned that someone we love is terribly ill and all we know, all we want, is to be there, present, for and with them. Or maybe we sense it at the end when someone is dying. Suddenly, there's no room for expectations or judgments or grudges or improvement. All there is, is being with that person in this moment, now, however imperfect it is.

To rest naked in the now, we will strip away that which keeps us from being present through easy practices you can do at home, or on a walk, alone or with a friend or partner. The process will not involve a struggle, but will come naturally, like what happened in Aesop's fable, "The North Wind and the Sun." These two characters had a bet as to who could remove a traveler's coat first. The North Wind howled and whipped, grabbing at the edges, trying to rip the coat off the man, but the traveler only clutched it tighter. The sun, on the other hand, just kept beaming a warm light. As the traveler relaxed in the warm and inviting environment, he naturally took off his coat.

Like Aesop's traveler, we are embarking on a journey of letting go. We are setting off to peel away layers of conditioning, not to gain new knowledge. The process is *not* about

- self-improvement (in the traditional senses),
- bettering your circumstances,
- thinking your way out of something, or
- fixing your problems.

It is about what happens when you stop doing all that and rest in naked awareness. We are letting go of what we think so we can discover what is left: our own intrinsic purity; goodness through and through. That is what you'll uncover. Everything else pales in comparison.

Chapter 2

Getting Lucky

Rest is not idleness, and to lie sometimes on the grass under a tree on a summer's day, listening to the murmur of the water, or watching the clouds float across the sky, is by no means a waste of time.

—J. Lubbock

When I was a small child we lived in a modest suburban neighborhood in Bellevue, Washington. The street was lined with small three- or four-bedroom ramblers of varying shapes interspersed with a few split-level homes. Immediately out our back door to the left stood a rabbit hutch with our pet albino rabbit, Hidey. The backyard featured a grassy little hill that flattened out and butted up against a rock wall embankment. To one side of the little plateau, my parents had built a wood deck. Out front, a grassy lawn graced the sidewalk; low bushes lined the house and a couple of trees stood sentinel in the side yard.

I lived in this house from age one to seven. This is where I learned to read *Winnie-the-Pooh* and how to ride a tricycle. It's where I followed the big kids on bikes on my trike, as they rode down the steep hill behind my house and swooshed to a stop above the embankment, while I, brakeless, launched off the edge and crash-landed. It's where I went to preschool and kindergarten, where I wore a skeleton costume for Halloween, where I helped my mother iron shirts for my dad, where I annually watched *The Wizard of Oz* and trembled in fear at the bad witch and flying monkeys.

Most important of all, this house is where I first experienced unmitigated awe and where I embraced the simple joy of seeking, without knowledge or expectation... and without fear of being bored.

My world was mostly predictable, until one day, someone told me that four-leaf clovers brought you luck and were quite rare, but if persistent, you might find one. Searching for something precious and rare became my favorite solo game. In the front yard on any given sunny day, I settled myself down for the long haul on "grass" speckled with clovers. I sat there happily with the warm sun on my back for hours looking at all the clovers. Patiently, my small hands separated each little clover, one from the next, examining it to determine if it had three or four leaves. Again and again, I moved from one three-leafed clover to the next, not dwelling on any single clover. Just noting it and moving on.

Unknowingly, I was practicing a negation technique Buddhists call *Neti neti*—"not this, not that." I would sit undistracted and focused for hours as I searched for four-leaf clovers. Sometimes, I'd go inside and grab a snack or some lemonade and head back out again. I had no expectation that it would be easy or fast. In fact, I knew I needed diligence—otherwise everyone would have four-leaf clovers, I reasoned. But maybe, maybe if I persisted and just kept looking, maybe one day I would find one... and eventually I did. But the process of searching was always enough. I was discovering firsthand the joy of mindfulness. It was always enough to sit and quietly keep looking, undistracted and still—at peace with the process itself. One day, I looked up and saw a rainbow for the first time. That such unexpected beauty could just appear out of thin air stopped me entirely. I was awestruck.

But somewhere in the process of growing up, my natural mindfulness—the part of me that enjoys the process more than the outcome—got lost. Though I might not have been able to name it, I felt its loss. It is part of what drove me to seek for more—more *what*, at that time, I wasn't sure, but I felt a longing for it just the same. Years later, I read a book by Buddhist teacher Cheri Huber titled *That Which You Are Seeking Is Causing You to Seek*. What was causing me to seek was the natural sense of presence that is unconditionally loving, at peace with the process of living, and not focused on or judging the outcome.

Eventually, as an adult I decided to do something about this loss. I decided to learn to meditate. I had heard it could quiet your mind and add peace and joy to your life. I knew I needed that. I imagined I had to get rid of my thoughts in order to meditate, which simultaneously sparked fear: fear of boredom and fear of failing to meditate correctly—a common response. Like most adults, I had been conditioned to habitually think, to believe my thoughts are what bring meaning and appreciation to my life, to imagine that I experience life through thinking about it. Also, like others, I had been conditioned to go after what I wanted, to *strive* for success. I immediately turned meditating into a task, something to be learned and to perfect, but I also instinctively saw the flaw—how does one succeed in going after a quiet and peaceful mind when one is beset with thoughts?

Although I will forever appreciate my first meditation teacher for introducing me to the concept of meditation, I wish instead of underscoring the idea that I needed to get rid of my thoughts to actively seek peace, that she had pointed me back to my childhood. I wish she had told me that meditation was less like a grown-up perfecting the next skill and more like a relaxed child at play, enjoying the process of searching for four-leafed clovers, periodically and unexpectedly awestruck by something else altogether, something precious and ineffable that fills you with natural joy, like a rainbow.

Even better, she might have told me meditation is fun and relaxing, too, especially if you approach it less like taking on new work and more like seducing a lover...

Chapter 3

Slipping into Something More Comfortable

Won't you excuse me for a moment while I... slip into something a little bit more... comfortable?
—Madeline Kahn, *Blazing Saddles* (1974)

When you come to the end of a long day of work and your shoes are pinching your feet, your waistband feels uncomfortably tight, and you yearn for something less restrictive—something that signals it's the end of the busy day—you may loosen your tie or slip off your shoes so you can relax.

In the same way, you can prepare yourself to meditate—to be present. You can take a moment to transition between the typical mind-fueled, agenda-propelled activity of our days and the nothingness of pure rest. I like to take a few moments to make sure my physical environment is warm and inviting. I might even lie down for a few minutes, idly watching out a window or maybe listening to some soft music. I breathe deeply and allow a playful inner smile to emerge, as if I had just turned to my inner lover-self and said, "Do you mind if I slip into something more comfortable?"

For me, approaching meditation this way dissipates the panicky feeling of always having to "do" something. I begin to breathe a little deeper and more easily, as if I have just removed uncomfortable clothing—clothing that serves a purpose in certain situations, like a crisp business suit worn to an important meeting, but clothing that would now inhibit me from fully relaxing.

Two-minute transition practice

This is what I recommend you do mentally before any awareness practice: toss off the "pinching shoe" thoughts and the "to-do list" jacket; toss on a light, attractive, "barely there" mind robe; and acknowledge your readiness to be naked with your lover-self: open, vulnerable, inviting, and present, like a deep sigh in the arms of your lover.

Rest for a moment quietly, easily. No agenda.

Even two minutes of resting the body in such an environment—of doing nothing—will change your perspective and signal to yourself that you are ready to peel off the day's thought streams—to be ready and attentive to something else altogether. That something is what I like to think of as intimacy with the moment.

We meditate because, in the deepest longing of our heart, we want to be stripped of everything—to go "naked through the gate," as my teacher Joel Morwood puts it.

In the pages that follow, you and I are going to practice getting naked and intimate with the moment. Whenever you reach to open these pages, take a luxurious moment to ready yourself for the transition. This readiness is like one finger gently tracing the outline of your inner lover-self's face... contented and ready for more.

These days meditation seems to have entered the realm of "shoulds." We hear so much about the benefits of it that we end up thinking we *should* do it rather than recognizing our heart's desire to be still and quiet some of the time. As a "should do" item, we add it to our list of things we'll get to "one of these days" but never quite manage to. Of course, this is understandable. When you are filled with worrisome thoughts and an already long to-do list, sitting down and doing nothing not only sounds daunting and overwhelming but also like a weary waste of time. But the upshot is we get turned off by the idea of meditation before we have the chance to get turned on.

So, let's do something different right from the start. Perfect for a "no-self self-help" book, the following practices are not meditations so much as gentle awareness practices. So, let's not think about meditating at all. Instead, we will begin by relaxing the body.

Relaxing the body is the most important lesson I've learned, and its practice is one I use every day of my life to bring me back to the present. Full-body relaxation runs counterintuitive to all our conditioning. Society teaches us to earnestly go after what we want. If we want a peaceful mind, we think we need to strive for it. Thus, when we are full of thoughts and worries, our instinct is to think we must be failing and should try harder — *meditate* more earnestly — to get rid of them. In fact, the exact opposite is true. When we are restless, feeling unsettled, and stuck in an active mind, what we actually need to do is expend *less* effort, not more. If I could choose only one word to sum up the entirety of my twenty-five years of awareness practice, I would say this: relax.

We may think that we need to relax the mind to relax the body, but again, the reverse is true. When we relax the body, the mind naturally relaxes. Like the mother at my retreat, we are going to "settle" our bodies. As we do so, bringing attention to each body area, you will find that the body is a powerful tool for bringing us directly to the present moment.

In our first awareness practice, we essentially will cultivate the effect we get when we take two weeks off from everything, arrive at an exotic beach, plunk down in a lounge chair with an umbrella-laden drink in hand and a warm, just-right breeze wafting through, and let out a huge sigh. We are going to build a mini-vacation into our day.

Just ten minutes, that's all we need.

Today, right now, we are going to practice lovingly, curiously, happily, intentionally relaxing amidst all our chaos.

Are you ready? Are you ready to commit to a ten-minute vacation that will form a foundation for joyful, ecstatic living? Say "yes."

Say yes, because you can feel that big plop-on-a-lounge-chair sigh in your heart now, that moment of being alive and free, that sudden insight or remembrance that life is not a business to be managed, but a mystery by which to be awestruck. Say yes, because a commitment signals to ourselves that we have made something a priority.

Making a commitment

Now that you've said yes, take one bolder step. Right now, decide what your commitment to your mini-vacation will be. How many days per week will you take a ten-minute vacation? How many weeks in a row? (Hint: aim for at least three weeks.) Remember, it does not have to be grandiose. It can be as simple as ten minutes per week, or ten minutes three times per week, over a one-month period. The important thing is that it is something you can easily do.

Write it down below. Make a sign and keep it where you can easily see it. Set a calendar alert or alarm on your phone to help remind you.

It's your first experiment. You get to judge it for yourself and record how it affects you. Remember to be gentle and encouraging to yourself. Give yourself a little internal "high five" each time you meet your commitment. It's hard to start a new habit. In this practice, and all the practices in this book, we only use carrots, no sticks.

My commitment

I commit to take a ten-minute vacation _____ times a week for _____ weeks, and to take notes about how I feel and what I noticed.

Well done!

I congratulate you for taking the first step on a juicy adventure sure to enliven your heart. Remember, the goal is not to feel any certain way, only to notice how we are in the moment. I encourage you to embark on this journey with the curious eye of a child and the investigative nature of a detective or scientist to discover what makes *you* feel better. You'll be glad you did!

You might want to dedicate a journal to the process (or write directly in this book). It's helpful to take notes. What worked for you? What didn't? How did a practice make you feel? What came up for you?

Next, you'll find four awareness practices to help you jump into the juicy now. There is nothing to perfect here. No goal to be obtained. Just an opportunity to relax and observe.

By the way, most of the practices in this book are available as guided meditations. I am working on an online class that will include most of the practices in this book. The first four practices are available for free as audio recordings on my website (https://marijkemccandless.com), if you prefer to have me walk you through the practices. Or, you can record these practices yourself by reading them into a recorder (most smartphones have one) and then listening to yourself talk through the practice.

Let's practice!

Practice #1: Kissing Yourself All Over

Let's take a little vacation to a waterfall of warm, golden light, accessible right here, right now. I like to think of this waterfall as kissing yourself all over.

The practice:

- Take a moment to tune in to your body. You can be sitting or lying down, whatever feels comfortable to you. Center yourself by intentionally breathing a little deeper for two or three breaths, but essentially do nothing for a moment or two.
- Now draw all your attention up to the top of your head and imagine, if you will, that there is a waterfall of soothing, warm, playful golden light cascading down your head. Moving slowly, like liquid gold or honey, the harmless golden light covers your skull and drips slowly down to your eyebrows, your nose, and the tops of your ears.
- As the soothing light touches each part of your head, it magically releases all tension and allows that part to relax. Now you feel the warm golden light on your cheeks and the back of your neck. An odd tingling accompanies the light, moving from inside the body outward, caressing the cheekbones and causing you to smile slightly as it reaches your lips. Like honey, the light curves under your chin, soothing your neck and shoulders, and now relaxes your shoulder blades.
- Everywhere the light has touched is more relaxed than before, as if the light accepts everything that it touches, not judging, not recoiling, not worrying, just embracing. There is a feeling of ease, like when you slip into a hot bubble bath, that accompanies the liquid light as it glides

down your body. You watch as it inches down your upper arms, touching your heart inside, releasing the frozen feeling sometimes stored there. You can feel your chest grow warm. The liquid light is friendly and nurturing, gently cascading down and around your arms, into your armpits, down your torso, over your hands and around each finger.

- The light continues down, now reaching your navel, coating your back. You can feel the tension in your spine melting. Sometimes, as the light touches a sensitive spot, a bit of pain flares up, as if the area has long been ignored and is a little stiff as it begins to wake up.

- Every discrete part of your body is touched by the light, as it continues to move like honey down your lower belly, down your tired hips, between your legs, seeking anyplace needing attention, needing release. It travels down the thighs, pausing at the knees to circle and penetrate before moving down your lower legs, loosening tight calf muscles, encircling the ankles, and at last covering your entire foot and each toe.

- Rest now, with warm golden light coating you. This light is the attention of your awareness, and just like the effect of kissing an "ouchy" better, each time we bring the power of our attention to our body, we enliven it.

- Sages teach that a relaxed, happy body cultivates a relaxed, happy mind—that mind follows body. My experience has proven their wisdom to be true. But you don't need to take my word for it. Don't believe me. Don't blindly trust me. Instead, experiment for yourself. Discover for yourself its truthfulness. What happens in your body/mind when you systematically pay attention and relax your entire physical body?

What was this experience like for you? Jot a few notes about your experience right now, while it is fresh.

Notes:

_____

_____

_____

_____

_____

_____

_____

_____

_____

Practice #2: Following the Breath of the Beloved

I am going to introduce to you the sweetest breath-related awareness practice that I know. This technique is one that I devised on my own, when I found myself frustrated by breath meditations. Everywhere teachers and practitioners raved about simple breath meditation. "Just notice the breath," the guides said. But the instruction didn't work for me. I come from a long history of mantra meditation and have had a rough journey cottoning on to using the breath. Eventually, I tracked down what was hanging me up and devised my own technique, which now quickly brings me to a sublime state.

When I focused on my breath, I noticed no matter how much I tried not to, I subtly "controlled" my breath. As soon as I brought my attention to the breath, I unconsciously began controlling it. I became curious what was actually happening in my body. I wondered what was the physiological reason for this? Why was it that from one moment to the next my body went from happily breathing on its own, to my feeling like I needed to control it—even when I didn't want to?

I hadn't studied anything about the human body in years, so I began researching. I learned that there are two breathing centers in the body. One is the *involuntary* center, controlled by the brainstem, which autonomically causes the body to breathe all day long without thought or attention, and the other is the *voluntary* breathing control center, located in the cerebral cortex—the thinking part of the brain.

I had an a-ha moment realizing that somehow, I was triggering the voluntary breathing center. In other words, instead of purely watching, my mind was engaged and thinking. I was approaching breath meditation as something "to do." I was actively, albeit subconsciously, going after something.

As I paid close attention while on retreat, I realized that my attention was slightly but perpetually being pulled into the future. I was grasping—just a little. So, again and again, I started over, slowing down, practicing *following* rather than leading the breath.

I continued to struggle.

Now, I was familiar with the power and practice of controlled breathing in awareness practice. There are all kinds of different voluntary breathing techniques, such as Pranayama, which is essentially intentional breath control (see Appendix A). These are helpful and can strengthen the connection between mind and body. I love and appreciate Pranayama, but I was interested in letting go of control completely. I wanted to see if I could simply watch my breath without helping it at all, but not ignoring it either.

I began to experiment. I remembered a time when my husband had been quite sick. I rested with him and as a way of being as present and close to him as possible I closely watched his breath and matched my own to his. I had to stay completely present, just watching, in order to match his breath, as I had no knowledge or expectation as to when his next breath was coming. Because he was sick, his breath was ragged and uneven. I had to pay close attention and in order to match his, I couldn't be even a little ahead. In this capacity, without even consciously thinking about it, I was practicing the art of witnessing—a powerful adjunct to awareness practice, but one I had not successfully applied to breath meditation yet.

It dawned on me to do this with myself. In the scenario with my husband, I was practicing witnessing breathing that was out of my control. This was the attitude I wanted to adopt with myself. So, I imagined that I was my own lover and that I was following my lover's breath. This had an immediate and noticeable effect. Grasping—i.e., imagining and attempting to control the future—left. If I was truly just witnessing the breath of my beloved (me) as it happened, there was no control even possible. The voluntary breathing mechanism located in the cerebrum was not triggered. Breathing just happened. I followed. The result was astounding, as I and the inner beloved breathed as one.

Here's the thing: breath only happens precisely in the present moment—now.

By paying attention to the breath, happening on its own, I can directly experience the present moment, but only right now—and only if I am following it without any knowing or expectation.

I encourage you to try this sweet exercise.

Think of this as a two-part practice. Begin by first practicing witnessing the breath of another. This does not have to be a human other; it could also be a pet.

All by itself, this witnessing of the breath of another is a powerful and sweet way to get present. A friend of mine, Marni, did this with her cat and reported it to be what she called "very witnessy."

That is what we are going for.

Let's practice!

Part 1: Being with the breath of another

To do this, get completely comfortable, even lying down next to your beloved pet (or human) friend. Your companion does not even have to know what you are doing for this exercise to be effective.

The practice:

- Allow your physical body to feel completely at ease. This is not an exercise that requires a strict posture. Our aim is to feel completely physically relaxed.
- Just rest quietly for a moment, no agenda.

- Gently bring your attention to simply notice the breathing of your beloved companion.
- Just notice the rise and fall of their chest for a few moments.
- Nothing more to do, just notice.
- Breath goes in, chest rises, breath goes out, chest falls.
- In and up, out and down.
- Next, intentionally bring your own breath in alignment with theirs. Allow your breath to match theirs. In this part of the practice you will be utilizing your own voluntary breathing center, so don't worry about which breath system is being triggered. The intention of this exercise is to practice following a breath that is absolutely beyond your control. It's like developing a muscle memory, experiencing what it feels like to breathe without any knowing or expectation of when the next breath might come.
- Continue matching your breath with the beloved for a few minutes, breathing together. Notice what it feels like to be that closely tuned in with another—breathing at the same rate as them.
- This little practice is a simple yet profound way of being present with them.
- Notice, too, what it feels like to witness the breath, to have breath be your entire focus for a few minutes.
- Remember, breath only happens precisely in the present moment—now.
- This is a taste of the experience of Now—just being with the breath of another.
- Practice noticing and matching the breath of another whenever you think of it. Enjoy it—know that you can't do it wrong. If your attention wanders and you forget what you are doing, it's no problem. In fact, it is natural and expected. You simply start over.

- We tend to judge ourselves when we do not sustain attention. But the practice is not about whether or not we sustain attention, it's about developing the ability to redirect attention once you notice it has wandered. And it's not a race or a marathon. It's just practice. You can dip in for just minutes at a time—a little game you play with yourself. A challenge to spend one minute a day noticing and breathing with your cat. No big deal, just a sweet minute together in the now.
- Take a moment here to jot down what this experience is like for you.

Notes: _____

_____

_____

_____

_____

_____

_____

Part 2: Being with your own breath
as if it were the Beloved

When you are ready or if you become curious (keeping in mind that there is no need to move on) try it with your own self. Practice resting as if you are your own Beloved and you want nothing more than to match your breath so that you are completely present with yourself.

We forget sometimes, but we each *are* our most reliable beloved companion. This technique is a way to deeply befriend, accept, and be with yourself exactly in this moment no matter what else is going on. The practice only requires willingness and focus. Even if done for only a few minutes, it is a welcome relief to paying attention to the persistent nattering of the mind. You might look forward to these sweet moments of undistracted devoted time to be present with yourself in the simplest, sweetest of ways.

The practice:

- Again, begin this practice totally at ease. Allow your body to be comfortable.
- This practice can be a wonderful exercise at night just after you turn out the lights, or if you wake in the middle of the night.
- Just rest quietly for a moment, no agenda.
- Now, remember what it felt like when you tuned in to the breath of your companion, just noticing their chest rising and falling. Remember that feeling of "witnessing" another. Notice that when we are witnessing another our attention is directed there. We are not caught up in our thoughts as much. We have directed attention away from our thoughts to focus on the breathing of another.
- Now, in this moment, we are going to direct our attention to the natural rise and fall of our own breath.
- Easy.
- No rush.
- Relax your eyes. During this practice, play with closing your eyes, or opening them half-mast; diffuse seeing, soft downward gaze, just enough so that from the corner of your eye you might see your chest rise.
- Relax your eye sockets.
- Relax your cheeks.
- Notice when you relax your cheeks, attention drops.

- Allow your attention to drop, sinking gently into the chest cavity, away from the head.
- Allow your attention to simply notice your breathing, endeavoring to follow it, just like you followed the breath of another.
- As attention follows the breath, there is no grasping, no inside knowledge of when the next breath is coming, no controlling.
- Attention is simply following the breath as it arises. Alert passivity.
- Chest rises, shoulders rise a little.
- Chest falls, shoulders drop.
- Notice what it feels like in a moment when pure witnessing happens, when you don't trigger the voluntary breath center to take over.
- This is an endlessly patient practice.
- There is no hurry.
- You can't do it wrong.
- You just keep practicing noticing, as if your breath was that of another.
- Every breath is another opportunity to simply notice.
- Every breath is right now.
- As you make this practice your own, don't be afraid to experiment. Try slightly different positions. You can try a formal posture sitting up straight, feet touching the floor, or try reclining, even slouching, or just lie down completely.
- Experiment with your hands too, leaving them at your side or perhaps gently clasping them over your abdomen or against your heart region, so that your hands sense the gentle rise and fall of the torso.
- Remember, every breath can happen on its own without our intervention.

- And we *can* develop the knack of just watching it, and when we do there is a sweetness present, a brightening, a stillness that pervades all. You might detect a kind of surreal feeling or an electricity in the air.
- This is presence.
- This is you.
- This is Now.
- Take a moment to write about what the experience was like, what you noticed.

Notes: _____

_____

_____

_____

_____

_____

_____

_____

_____

Practice #3: What Else Is Here?
(A Sensory Awakening Experience)

This next awareness practice is my own personal secret weapon for smiting the horrible voices in my head that natter all day long about what I *should* be doing; constantly analyzing, comparing, judging; always looking for what is wrong, and what is not enough.

It's not their fault, really—those voices in my head are just my brain doing its job as best it can, always endeavoring to improve, to protect, to gather more data.

We talked about this early on. We are wired to suffer. Turns out, that is never going away. It is not the job of those voices to be satisfied with what is, not their job to be content. It is their job to constantly scan for trouble, to be vigilant.

Our job, on the other hand, is to discover that we are not only those thoughts.

We are something infinitely more, something that is content and at ease, something full of wonder and awe for life in all its forms. Something that the thoughts are a subset of, not the master of.

One of my favorite metaphors for the thoughts that can run helter-skelter in my mind, controlling me, hijacking my face, is to recognize them as something like a willful puppy: excitable, out of control, full of energy, hungry—adorable sometimes— but hyperactive and prone to accidents. I can easily appreciate that a puppy needs to be trained to keep it from running wild, pooping and peeing anywhere, shredding the furniture, and barking loudly at every noise.

Such it is with our thoughts. We need to show them who is master. We need to be able to take a break from listening to our puppy-like thoughts. We need to encourage them sometimes to sit and stay, to recognize what is actual danger so that they are not barking at every potential hazard no matter how remote. Sure, we need to listen and play with them *sometimes,* but not *all* the time.

After all, thoughts are only one of the phenomena that make up this sensual complex being.

I have found the easiest way to begin breaking the willful demands of our thoughts is to simply divert attention away from them by actively focusing on the senses instead of the thinking mind.

I developed a code phrase to help me do just that: "What else is here?"

When I find that my thoughts have consumed me and are spinning a story that I am no longer enjoying—when I find myself in a state of suffering (however mild or dramatic that might be)—I know it is time for my secret weapon.

I love my secret weapon because it doesn't require anything special at all. I can be anywhere, doing anything. I don't need to be in a quiet place or on a meditation cushion. All I need to do is take a simple break—a little vacation—and ask myself: What else is here?

And by that, I mean, what else is here *besides my thoughts*?

This is my code phrase to immediately tune in to my senses.

The practice:

- Right now, we are going to take a little break, a little vacation designed to awaken our senses to notice all the different kinds of phenomena that can arise in our awareness—sight, sound, taste, touch, and smell. These deserve our attention and can provide us with a different, more immediate kind of awareness of our world than our thoughts can. Sensory experience only lives right now.

- So, right now let's look. Let's ask ourselves with the curiosity of a child: What else is here?
- Let's intentionally and systematically focus on each one of our senses.
- Close your eyes and relax for a breath or two.
- Draw your attention entirely to what you hear.
- What sounds are arising and passing away as you listen?
- Notice them.
- Don't worry about capturing every single one of them, just notice the sounds that naturally capture your attention. Notice the uniqueness of each sound, how some arise and pass away, how some seem to be more persistent, like background noise.
- Just notice the sounds of this moment.
- Allow that passive-alert attention to be watchful, wondering, curious; what sound might arise and pass away?
- Now, bring your attention to physical sensations—to touch.
- Notice the intersection between your body and whatever it is resting on: a chair, the floor.
- It can be a powerful exercise itself to deliberately draw all attention down to the feet. To feel them resting on a surface, to tune in to each toe.
- Notice, too, any other bodily sensations that might capture your attention: a sore neck, dry eyes.
- Notice that the thinking mind will often pipe up trying to pin down the reason for the physical sensation, such as "I wonder if my eyes are dry because I am allergic to ragweed." Instead of thinking about the sensation, endeavor to precisely describe the physical sensation itself.

- "My eyes feel raw, mildly scratched, and I am aware of the pressure of my eyelid as it brushes over my eye with each blink. There is a dull ache behind the eye, a tired feeling."

- In this way we begin to disassociate the sensory experience from our thoughts *about* the sensory experience. We begin to practice recognizing the difference.

- Move on now to taste. Focus all your attention on the sensation of taste. Is there the lingering taste of coffee still in the mouth? Is there any noticeable taste at all?

- Similarly, focus on the sensation of smell. Breathe in deeply through the nose. Notice anything you might smell. Look for subtle smells, like the vaguely metallic smell of air conditioning. Or perhaps there are more vivid smells arising, like dinner cooking. Just pay attention for a moment to whatever you might smell.

- Finally, we are going to slowly open our eyes, noticing the visual phenomenon that is before us. Notice how quickly the mind will label what it sees: computer, monitor, desk. Gently move your eyes around, just noticing how different visual phenomena arise. Allow a sense of wonder to arise as if seeing your environment for the first time—like when we travel to a new country and are all wide-eyed with awe at the extraordinary or unusual sights we see—sights that to another may be their mundane world.

- So, that's it.

- The quickest way out of the barking puppy-dog mind—back to now—is to deliberately bring attention to the senses. To ask: What else is here?

- This whole exercise needn't take long, just a few minutes to reset ourselves, and get re-grounded in right Now.

- Take a moment to write about what the experience was like, what you noticed.

Notes: _____

_____

_____

_____

_____

_____

_____

_____

Practice #4: Prayer in the Heart
(Awakening Naked Desire for the Divine)

This awareness practice is derived from the very first sustained practice I learned. The version I learned consisted of a series of mantras or affirmations that I would repeat while sitting quietly.

I was on a weekend workshop and we were learning a series of four techniques. I had been trying hard all weekend to pay attention to the rules and how to do the practices perfectly. I worried I wasn't doing it right. I worried I wasn't getting it. I worried the practices and teachings were too esoteric and not made for my normal suburban lifestyle. I thought perhaps it was all a waste of time.

Between Saturday night and Sunday, I developed an almost debilitating migraine as I tried to do the practice and worried all night. In the morning I decided to return even though my head was pounding—I thought I better finish and then reassess.

That day, we learned the third technique, a simple heart-centered practice, and after ten minutes my entire world shifted—all the pain fled from my body and head and I entered into the most spacious experience of my life to that point. As my awareness expanded, I felt uninhibited joy and love. I had the sensation that I could feel the spaces between the atoms that made up my body—and those spaces were vast. It was a truly awe-inspiring moment that completely shifted my understanding of what was possible. It got my attention and woke something up inside me that I had no mental understanding about.

At the time, I thought what I was learning was a unique and special practice, but learned later that focusing attention like this on a short prayer, mantra, or affirmation in the heart is practiced around the world.

The original practice I learned was a bit complicated with lots to remember. What I share here is an abbreviated version that I have found works just as well.

The critical component that all versions share has to do with getting quiet and choosing a word or phrase that captures either your deepest longing or your most transcendent feeling of wonder or awe. I call this the "awe" word.

In selecting this word or short phrase, however, you must be careful that there is no hidden baggage associated with the word. So, for instance, some people take great comfort in the word "God," while for others "God" carries a confusing or even negative message.

You must select something that feels positive to you. Common single words might be "love," "beauty," "truth," "beloved." But I can tell you that my original first choice was a mouthful: "evolving consciousness," because it held for me a vision of great potential. On the other hand, when we taught this technique to our seven-year-old daughter, she chose "crepes," as her most revered word of the moment.

You might also come up with a short phrase, if you prefer. There are many ready-made versions that different religions encourage. Christian versions often include the Jesus Prayer: "Jesus Christ, Son of God, have mercy upon me, a sinner," or the start of the St. Francis Prayer: "Lord, make me an instrument of your peace." In India there are lots of different short mantras such as the Kashmiri Shaivism mantra: *Om Namah Shivaya.* The Sufis practice their own version of a short prayer, called *dhikr,* where they repeat *Allah, Allah, Allah.*

Whatever your word or phrase, you must take a moment to select it. Keep it light and easy—no stress, just a word or phrase that brings joy or awe to your heart, in the same way a pretty sunset does.

There might be a tendency for the mind to want to switch from word to word, searching for the "perfect" one. That's just monkey mind. Let it go. Pick one and let your mind know gently that you are going to try this one for a while and if it doesn't work, you can change it later, if you like. Mine has morphed several times over the years and currently is "My Beloved."

During a single session, however, you need to settle on one selection.

When we first start, all we are going to do is repeat our awe word for a set amount of time—say, five or ten minutes. We set a timer and silently repeat our word. If we forget what we are doing for a while during the timed period, that's okay. We just return our attention to repeating our word.

There are a few additional and some optional steps I'll talk about here, before we practice.

You can decide eventually whether to keep your eyes closed or open, but to start, we will close our eyes.

You also can choose to synchronize your awe word with your breath, silently saying it on the out breath, for instance, and then remaining silent on the in breath (or vice versa). Or use some other method of counting as you go, such as prayer beads or a rosary.

After you have practiced with the word alone for a while, we want to add the heart element by bringing your attention down to your heart as you practice. To do that, simply imagine the word or words resting quietly in your heart during the session. Don't worry if you can't actually visualize this, just have the intention for it to rest there. Allow your attention to move to the heart center while you are repeating your word or words.

If you like, as I do, you may add the word "Om" to your awe words(s): "Om My Beloved," for instance. But it is not necessary. I do it because I like the physical sensation of saying the word "Om." For whatever reason, I feel this word in my chest.

To make it easier to draw attention to your heart center, you may also place your hands on your heart while you practice. It is not necessary, just nice.

As you practice, allow your attention to sink deeper into the heart space, the word resonating deep inside the chest as it moves in and out with the breath.

Let's try this powerful prayer in the heart and see for ourselves what the mystics of all the religions have found when using this simple practice to touch into our deepest longing and our innate sense of awe: it can open your heart to the great mystery of Life—to the Beloved.

We will sample some of the different options during this guided meditation. On your own you can choose what you like best.

The practice:

- First let's bring our attention right here, right now to the moment. Feel how your body meets the chair or floor, notice your quiet breath moving in and out.

- Close your eyes and get comfortable. Let your hands rest in your lap, gently nestled against each other. Just rest for a moment, allowing distractions to fall away, allowing yourself to anticipate the mystery unfolding.

- Now, I invite you to come up with an awe word or words. Something that captures simply your longing for the divine, or your sense of awe and wonder. Something that brings you peace or joy.

- Something with no baggage. You might use something traditional like God or Jesus or Krishna or Allah or something more spiritually generic like Universe, Divine Mother, or Great Spirit. Or perhaps something more secular like Truth or Beauty. It can be anything—it only needs to be something that resonates in your heart.

- I'll give you a moment to settle on a word or phrase.
- Okay, now focus your attention on your breath for a few moments. Notice the breath going in and going out. Just notice. Breath goes in, chest rises, breath goes out, chest lowers.
- Breathe in.
- Breathe out.
- Breathe in.
- Breathe out.
- Now bring your word or phrase to mind and let's gently synchronize it with our breath.
- Breathe in silently.
- Breathe out the word or phrase.
- Breathe in silently.
- Breathe out the word or phrase.
- As you move through this practice, thoughts may come in a never-ending stream. They might be commenting on what you are doing or judging what you are doing. They might be thinking about what to make for dinner. Don't worry about it. It is perfectly normal. Thoughts come and go. Just draw your attention gently, kindly back to your word or phrase when you notice that you've become distracted.
- You can decide if you like the added movement of touching prayer beads or fingers as you say your word or phrase with your breath. Either way, keep practicing until your attention becomes calm.
- Now we are going to bring our attention to our heart region. My teacher says that this is the area of your chest where your breath passes near your heart. You may place your hands on this area to help focus attention, but it is not necessary. Simply notice the heart region and the

breath passing through this region. Now add your word or phrase.

- Breathe in, silently noticing the breath passing through the heart region.
- Breathe out with the intention that the word or phrase is resting in the chest and touched by the breath as it passes.
- Breathe in, silently noticing the breath passing through the heart.
- Breathe out with the breath tickling the word or phrase resting in your chest.
- Continue to practice in this way, allowing your attention to sink deeper into the space inside your chest—a treasure chest where your word lives. Imagine the word is a whisper and you have to listen very carefully and sink ever deeper to hear its faint music as the breath enlivens it.
- Continue to practice in this way, allowing your attention to rest deep in the heart and then relax even more, silently saying the word to express the longing and devotion you feel.
- Bow in gratitude.
- Take a moment to write about what you noticed.

Notes: _____

_____

_____

_____

_____

_____

_____

_____

Chapter 4

Pillow Talk with the Beloved
(aka the Inner Guide)

*The Mentor I'm encouraging you to find is not a source of
permissive self-indulgence. Nor is the Mentor a hard taskmaster
who makes you do stuff you don't want to do for your own good.
The Mentor speaks from conscious compassionate awareness. The
Mentor, being center, loves you and all life unconditionally.*
—Cheri Huber

We've spent the last little while talking about awareness practices
that help us relax our body and mind—practices that put us
in touch with our hearts. These are important foundations for
feeling comfortable and at home in our bodies. They also help
us slow down so that we are not a victim of our racing thoughts
and judging minds. If we are going to get naked in the now, we
have to feel safe, relaxed, and at ease.

Imagine, if you will, the moment when a relationship turns
from a "let's grab a cup of coffee" friendship to "let's get
naked" together. There's something that happens at the pivot
point—a kind of reciprocal trust. Both parties are mutually
interested in showing more of themselves, in "baring" more
of themselves, if you will. The great body reveal is a trust
exercise because each one of us brings into the arena different
ideas on what a body should look like and how it should
perform. Will we meet up to our partner's standards? Will
they meet up to ours? Becoming physically intimate can be
an important aspect of growing closer together. Exposing
ourselves in this way also opens the door for another kind
of intimacy.

I'm talking about pillow talk—you know that easy, sweet kind of unguarded talk while cuddling where you feel safe to say whatever is on your mind. Typically, pillow talk happens just before or after sex and is different from either chatting over coffee or talking dirty. Pillow talk is where we get emotionally vulnerable and might tell deeply held secrets or dare to admit how much we love someone or lament about current personal challenges. Pillow talk is also where we learn that listening to our lover is as important as being heard ourselves. Pillow talk is important because it enhances emotional intimacy. It cements a friendship in a whole new way as sharing and being present with each other crosses boundaries both physical and emotional.

Pillow talk is also something we can and should do with ourselves—with our "inner" beloved. Just as we lovingly listen to and befriend others, we need to listen to and befriend ourselves, adopting an "I love you no matter what" attitude. We need to cultivate a safe space where we can first express what is going on, and second, listen to what is being said so that we can offer unconditional love and compassion back to ourselves.

This does not happen naturally in our busy lives. Rather, we tend to sprint from one goal to the next hoping that crossing something off our to-do list will bring us the inner satisfaction and peace we are seeking. But it never really does. And that is because the contentment we seek is something that does not rely on certain circumstances being met. The contentment comes from listening to and understanding that many things are out of our control and yet we are still deserving of love.

The easiest way to see what I mean is to imagine hanging out quietly with your lover or child or best friend and listening while they lament some of their struggles. You, as the listener in this scenario, might murmur little words of encouragement and maybe reflect on how challenging things seem for them at this moment, noting that you know they are doing the best they can in dealing with whatever life has delivered and acknowledging it can't be easy. In other words, you as a friend, a lover, or a parent will likely see them in their perfection, notwithstanding that things seem to be going wrong. You will hold space for the possibility that failure to reach the desired goal (degree, promotion, relationship) does not mean they have to settle for a life of discontentment. Your words will likely be gentle, kind, and understanding, but also not condescending or meaningless platitudes. You *do* see them as perfect—or possibly you accept them as imperfect but still worthy of love.

We all have the same inner loving wisdom available to offer ourselves, but we haven't all practiced being in touch with it. We can develop the knack, though, of being emotionally intimate and vulnerable with ourselves without censoring or judging ourselves. What we will discover when we do is a deep listening reservoir of sweet loving support for, and acceptance of, whatever is going on for us. We will discover that our inner beloved loves us exactly as we are and will help us be however we want to be.

If only we listen.

Buddhist teacher Cheri Huber has developed an entire practice around accessing this wise, loving inner beloved. She calls this inner source "the mentor." I love her definition of the mentor as "the centered awareness that allows us to observe and acknowledge conditioning without indulging in a self-hating reaction to it."

Yes. That's what we want to get in touch with—the centered awareness that understands we are subject to our conditioning and thus our challenges, and yet holds the possibility that we do not have to hate ourselves because of them. Rather we can open our arms and love that sweet being who is doing the best they can.

I like to think of this "mentor" as my inner beloved and when I think of interacting with my inner beloved conversationally, I think of pillow talk. Let's talk about some techniques you can try that allow yourself space to express whatever is going on without judging, filtering, editing, or controlling it. Access your authenticity without fear of looking bad, of not being the "right" person, not saying the "right" thing. Because once you get the knack of allowing everything to flow, you will find that love and compassion for yourself flow right in, too.

Let's practice!

Practice #5: Write Now Mind

Write Now Mind is a virtual writing group I developed to encourage people to commit to a weekly writing practice and to anonymously share their writing with others. In practice, it is so much more than those words describe.

The name *Write Now Mind* captures two concepts:

- a particular kind of timed "free-writing" practice that is uncontrolled and unfiltered, and
- a state of mind that pays attention to the particular moment at hand, which might include thoughts, feelings, and sensations.

The rules (inspired by Natalie Goldberg) for participating in *Write Now Mind* are simple.[i]

After setting a timer for ten minutes,

- keep your hand moving,
- be specific,
- lose control, and
- don't think.

What these rules mean is that we don't worry about grammar or punctuation. We don't filter or edit our writing. We travel wherever the pen (or keyboard) takes us, taboo or not. We are equally free to write the worst junk in the world and to be amazed at what comes out. We don't "try," we don't worry, we just write. When approached this way, writing can be fun and enlivening. We can let 'er rip!

When we engage in such a writing practice, we learn to pay attention to the details, to the particular sensations of the moment, but we also become familiar with what wants to be said, not what we think should be said. We get out of our judging, analytical, discursive mind and into the wilds within. In this way, we befriend our minds and ourselves. This teaches us to trust our voice and to begin to separate our unique expressions from our conditioned beliefs.

As readers, we learn to tune in to how certain words make us feel. We comment only on the positive and the particular details that caught our attention and describe what we found compelling about them. We are supportive and encouraging.

Being readers as well as writers allows us to practice both sides of the pillow talk. As writers, we fully express what wants to be said, and as readers, we carefully listen, encourage, and support—knowing full well how vulnerable it is to share raw, unfiltered, unedited thoughts.

Write Now Mind is a community formed without the aid of personal connection because we participate anonymously with one another. The anonymity allows us to let the words flow and creates a naturally safe harbor for our expression. Plus, since we all are doing it, we are naturally compassionate in our responses and feedback to others. More often than not someone writes what we were feeling. The reciprocated sharing allows us to accept and befriend our minds exactly as we find them and offers us the opportunity to see that the things we secretly believe are "wrong" with us are often universally experienced. This also creates a safe environment to be witnessed while being vulnerable—something like pillow talk.

In the years that I have been doing *Write Now Mind*, what I have seen and heard from people is that they had a lot of trepidation about putting their unedited words out, but that doing so and receiving encouragement has allowed them to begin to truly befriend themselves—to be more loving and kinder to themselves.

Freewriting in this way allows all the pent-up, confused, hiding-under-the-surface words to escape but without an agenda. Freewriting to a prompt differs from straight journal writing. In journal writing, we are intentionally reflecting on our life. In freewriting, you have no idea what might come out. It could be contemplative or it could be shallow—and that's the beauty of it. We get a chance to allow all of it. Sometimes the words that come out scream about frustration and being hurt or about the ways the author secretly believes they have failed in life. When the words are allowed to come out the author has a chance to hear them. Time and again, a softening happens, a clarity, a natural return to center. The things we are secretly terrified about are met with our own compassion and understanding, underscored as the group also reflects compassion and understanding. Equally powerful are the unbelievably sensitive, loving, kind thoughts that come pouring out unbidden. Our conditioning may have kept us from freely expressing how much we *love* life, and allowing those words to flow is incredibly powerful.

If you are curious about trying *Write Now Mind*, you are more than welcome. You can find details on my website. But it is also something you can do on your own, simply by becoming familiar with your mind and what wants to be said. If you do this, set a timer for ten minutes and randomly pick a prompt so that you don't have an opportunity to "think" about it beforehand. You can make a little jar of prompts. Write without stopping or thinking or editing or filtering for ten minutes. Take a little break, then go back and read what you wrote. You may even want to read it aloud. Then, as if you were offering feedback to an unknown participant, become a "reader" as well and offer that person—you—some encouragement and support. What did you find compelling about your response? What did you like? Remember, only positive support and encouragement are allowed.

The prompts that work best are incredibly simple. Here is a list for you to get started:

Right now, I notice...
I am longing for...
Home is...
I spent...
I see...
I delight in...
I remember...
I honor...
I know...
I don't know...
I should...
I shouldn't...
I think...
I don't think...
I feel...
I don't feel...
I aspire to...

Practice #6: Writing Your Way Home

I've been journaling since I was a child. My journal used to be where I would keep track of what I did on any given day. My childhood diaries say things like "Today, I went to the park with my best friend, Pam. We played on the swings. It was fun." Then, as a teenager, I would attempt to add emotion to my diary entries by adding exclamations and all caps: "We went to the roller rink for Friday night skating. There was a CUTE GUY!! He even smiled at me. I wonder if he will be back next week." As a young mother-to-be, I got more sophisticated and began adding specific details to my journals about my pregnancy as well as my hopes and dreams for my child. I talked directly to the fetus in my journals about how she moved and when.

When I went through my first serious adult crisis, however, I discovered that journaling could be much more than record-keeping. It was an avenue for releasing and expressing pent-up emotion. My journal became my best friend and in it, I could say anything. My journal was a safe harbor to talk and talk and talk (in writing). Years later, I describe in my memoir, *More... Journey to Mystical Union through the Sacred and the Profane*, just how valuable journaling had become for me in a chapter called "Writing My Way Home."

We all get lost sometimes, awash in overwhelming emotions that threaten to consume us. It is unimaginably helpful to have a safe space not only to let them out but to investigate them, to probe into our minds and heart. Going to a therapist can provide such a safe space; so, too, can a good friend, but sometimes those are not available or we're aware that our friend may not be able to take another emotional breakdown. We need to be able to help ourselves find our way back to the center.

Journaling has been that opening for me. It has allowed me to see deeper into my psyche. And its benefits are two-fold. First, journaling provides an outlet to let out whatever thoughts are brewing in my head, tormenting me. Just letting those thoughts land on a page instead of being stuck in my head helps a lot. But journaling has an even greater benefit than that.

Journaling also can show us repetitive themes in our life pointing to our conditioning that might be getting in the way of healing. I remember reading through my old journals—the kind where I had poured out all my frustration, everything that was wrong with my world, and my thinking that if only x, y, or z had happened, then all would be good. As I was reading, I came across the same words I had written many years before. *Exactly*.

At that moment, I saw that those words reflected a deep-seated, conditioned belief that life should be going differently. Reading those identical journal entries written during completely different times of my life brought out, in stark relief, that I kept getting stuck in the same line of thinking: there was something wrong that was unacceptable and I was suffering as a result.

This small moment was a pivotal one, for it forced me to acknowledge that my victim/righteousness conditioning was not serving me. It was not helping me grow or end suffering. I was forced to consider, if I was so right in my judgment of x, y, and z, why had my assessment not led me to peace?

After that realization, writing in and reading from my journals became a bit more like a striptease, unveiling a doorway to the subconscious. I began to realize that I was passionate about writing because it had the potential to expose me to Truth—even if it was something I did not want to see or believe about myself. Looking at the deepest and most vulnerable shadow sides of ourselves is not easy at first. We risk actively feeling shame or unworthiness or judgment from others. But in doing so, there is also the opportunity to unconditionally love ourselves.

On the flip side, while journaling has shown me what I fear and struggle with, journaling also has helped expose a tender and dear soul seeking not only to be understood but to understand others—a woman committed to accepting what is and to remaining compassionate no matter what.

Just as surely as journaling has exposed my shadows—my barriers to the world—it also has exposed my heart's desire to see below the surface to the naked purity of life and to spread that goodness.

Journaling paved the way to discovering my own writer's voice. I wrote in my journal about what I was seeing, feeling, or experiencing, and gradually, I began to see that different word choices made me feel differently.

Words are powerful tools that can make barriers or bridges—even to our inner well-being. Reading my writing allows me to experience the power of words. Words can engender a feeling of helplessness or empowerment. Words can be divisive and cutting or comforting and inspiring. Words can make me defensive or help me grow and change through hard times.

I began to choose more selectively which words I used, desiring to capture accurately what I was seeing, feeling, or experiencing. I played with more poetic ways of writing in my journal, using metaphor and simile to help describe how I was feeling. I no longer only wrote, "I'm sad." I went deeper, probing the nuances:

Sadness is flat and wet, a moldy towel, a flat seven-up, unsweetened chocolate, ash... or sadness can feel as full and passionate as an overripe peach, heavy like a brown banana.

—excerpt from *More... Journey to Mystical Union through the Sacred and the Profane.*

Journaling made me want to write better, and the desire to write well helped me develop a "writer's eye"—noticing and paying attention to precise details and patterns (instead of the cliché phrases we often rely on)—so that I could accurately capture what I was seeing and feeling.

Seeing the world through my writer's eye has a secondary benefit, too, for it also helps me cultivate the perspective of a witness, which in turn gives me some space from whatever drama is unfolding. That distancing ultimately helps me relax—something that is fundamental to inner peace. Writing can be a tool for communicating ideas to others, but I have found that writing, especially journal writing, is my most dependable way of finding my way home to the naked purity of my own heart.

There are all different kinds of journaling practices. Some suggest that you get up and write in a journal every day at the same time. It's true, that can be a powerful practice. What I am talking about is a little more selective. I am talking about journaling through pain when we feel lost. The next time you find yourself suffering, turn to a journal and pour your feelings out on paper. Just let it all out. All your frustrations, all your desires, all your hopes and dreams.

Tips for journaling your way home:
Date your entries.

You need not journal every day, but I have found it helps to date my entries or at least the journal itself. Later, sometimes years later, it helps to know what was going on in your life at the time of the entry to give it some context and grounding.

Focus on both the mental and physical feelings.

Often when we write we focus on what we are thinking, but it is a tremendously powerful practice to journal about physical sensations too. This teaches us to distance ourselves.

Describe the "problem."

What do you perceive to be "wrong" in your life right now? This can be very helpful in later identifying recurring themes in your life.

Go back and read your entries.

Read haphazardly—like dousing—just open up a page at random and read it.

Practice #7: Listening to Your Sweet Loving Voice

In the introduction to this chapter, I talked a little about Cheri Huber, a Zen Buddhist teacher who counsels her students to get in touch with what she calls the "mentor," which is what I refer to as the inner beloved. One of her techniques is called "recording and listening" (a tool she refers to as working out your own salvation diligently). I would like to pay homage to it here. Much like journaling, the process is about recording whatever is going on and then listening to it, but it has an added component that is fundamentally important and monumentally helpful: you record a response to that outpouring.

Let's say you find yourself supremely frustrated or emotionally distraught and you don't know what to do to get re-centered. Perhaps you are not drawn to writing. Instead, what you can do is pick up a recording device (most smartphones have a voice recorder built in) and speak all your frustrations out into the recorder. Just let it all out.

Then, you can listen—listen to that poor soul's (your) frustration or anguish. Listen as you would listen to your best friend who has come to you very upset, or like you would listen to a child. Listen as if it were not you.

Finally, make a new recording, talking directly to that person (you). Tell that person how much you love them, and how hard it must be to be going through whatever they are going through. Tell them that you are there to listen without judgment. Be your own best friend, seeing that person in their perfection notwithstanding their struggle. Life isn't always easy. We need to feel love. We can offer that unconditional love to ourselves. Below are steps for how to listen to your inner beloved.

The practice:

- Hold your recording device in your right hand and talk into it, saying exactly what you are feeling without holding anything back. Talk in the kind of way you might talk to a trusted friend or therapist. Let all your feelings and frustrations come out.
- Take a little break.
- Move the recorder into your left hand and listen to the recording. Listen carefully and attentively as if you were someone else, like your best friend or child who came to you pouring their heart out.
- Take a little break to absorb what you just heard, not only the words but the tone too.
- Now, turn on the recorder again and record whatever comes up naturally that might help or comfort the person you just listened to.
- Listen to the recording.
- Erase the first recording and listen only to the second one when stressed.
- Take a moment to write about what it was like to hear your own voice talking compassionately to yourself.

Notes: _____

_____

_____

_____

_____

_____

_____

_____

_____

Chapter 5

Getting to Know Yourself
(Including Your Thoughts)

One day just sit, close your doors, and write down for half an hour whatsoever is passing in your mind, and you will understand what I mean and you will be surprised what goes on inside your mind. It remains in the background, it is constantly there, it surrounds you like a cloud. With this cloud you cannot know reality; you cannot attain to spiritual perception. This cloud has to be dropped. And it is just with your decision to drop it that it will disappear. You are clinging to it — the cloud is not interested in you, remember, it.
—Osho (from the Mind card, Osho Zen Tarot deck)

Put your thoughts to sleep, do not let them cast a shadow over the moon of your heart. Let go of thinking.
—Rumi

Have you ever had a moment where you were stopped in your tracks by astounding beauty, for instance, such that your mind goes blank and nothing but the beauty of the moment consumes you?

Or, have you ever been so involved in an activity that you were no longer actively "thinking" about it but doing it in a state of natural flow?

Or, maybe, you have reached down to cuddle with a pet or child and been bowled over by an upwelling of sweet emotion that wipes out all else that is going on, and for that moment, you are only aware of the love between you.

These types of moments are examples of living naked in the now. One thing common to each scenario is that they are not marked by active thinking but rather by a different state—a non-thinking state.

When we tap into such moments, we naturally want that experience to last; such is the delight. Immediately the mind tells us that what we should seek is a state of no thoughts—a perfectly empty mind. We try and try to do this and get thwarted and discouraged.

"My mind is always thinking!" you might pronounce. "This path doesn't work for me. I can't get rid of my thoughts."

You would be right. In actuality, we can't get rid of our thoughts; they happen on their own as a natural consequence of having a brain. As I understand it, thoughts are electrochemical reactions that reflect every aspect of experience (interior and exterior)—our sensory and cognitive perceptions, as well as our ideas and beliefs about the world. There have been many claims about how many discrete thoughts a person has per day. Some (including Deepak Chopra and the National Science Foundation) say it's between 12,000 and 60,000. Recently, a neuroscience research team from Queen's University in Canada declared that a person typically has 6,000 thoughts per day. Either way, it doesn't matter for our exploration here. What's interesting is that thoughts are perpetually happening at a constant rate.

So, what happens when we experience moments of "no thought"? And how might we cultivate more such moments? That's what we will explore in our initiation into the self-inquiry process.

Ultimately, we will develop the knack of becoming awareness practitioners—tuned in to Life itself rather than our thoughts *about* life. To do so, we must, counterintuitively, dive deeper into the nature of thoughts and thinking.

Before we dive in, though, bear with me for a moment. I know you are anxious to practice. But words and phrases on the path can be tricky. You may think a particular term means one thing, whereas I have defined it differently. So, I'll take some time here to talk about what I mean when I refer to concepts such as "awareness," "conditioning," and "self-inquiry."

After I've defined the playing ground, we'll jump right in and get to know ourselves much better. Instead of ignoring our thoughts, we'll investigate everything about them, allowing them to arise and self-liberate while we watch. We'll get curious and ask ourselves questions as we notice the mind moving. When does a thought start and end? Where does it come from, and where does it go? Am I *what* I am thinking? Do I still exist when I am not thinking? What happens between thoughts? Can I be aware of my thoughts and not consumed by them? And we'll employ some practice tricks to help us.

Let's begin.

Awareness

Awareness is a term that I use a lot. I like to say that I am an "awareness practitioner," for instance. But it is a term that is not well-understood. It can even be a term that leads us down a completely different path.

When I first began investigating the nature of awareness, I used the more common meaning of awareness as knowledge or perception *of* a situation or fact. To me, being aware was something that I *did*. I believed (to become more aware) I needed to develop the skillset of cataloging more and more discrete phenomena. In short, I translated being an awareness practitioner to mean that I needed to be *more* vigilant than I already was. This effort to not miss anything, however, caused me stress.

As someone who had had PTSD, vigilance was already high on my list of conditioned responses. When triggered, I would drop into hyper-vigilance, jumping at noises, heart beating wildly, casting my attention in all directions, and perpetually scanning for danger. However, I now understand that being aware—in a spiritual sense—is something else altogether.

What I am now referring to when I talk about awareness is almost the opposite. You can sense it when instead of increasing your hyper-vigilance to phenomena that are arising, you soften your gaze and allow attention to spread in all directions without boundaries. You can sense it when you step back and become the observer rather than the doer.

When I talk about awareness, I am referring to something so simple, something that is always present and does not come and go. Some call it Presence or Beingness. Others call this non-conceptual underlying natural order of the Universe the Tao or the Way.

Lao Tzu, a philosopher/mystic from the sixth century BC, says, "The Tao is inexhaustible, limitless, the ancestor of all things. It is nowhere and everywhere. When we feel it as the source our separation diminishes, our beginning and our end become a part of something greater, mysterious and never-ending."

Many modern spiritual leaders also do their best to nod at what it means. Adyashanti says it is "that which is looking." Cheri Huber says it is "the intelligence that animates."

Eckhart Tolle tells us, "Awareness is beyond thinking. It's a space of consciousness where you can be the observer of your own mind—the awareness behind the thought processes."

I have also heard it described as receptive attention, especially when contrasted with deliberative thinking.

If this doesn't make perfect sense to you right now, that's okay. You don't have to understand awareness perfectly. Still, it helps to understand the direction of meaning when I refer to awareness—not ever-increasing hyper-vigilance, but a softening or relaxing into the underlying unchanging substrate of all of life happening right now.

Conditioning

We are going to dive into the nature of thoughts and thinking so that we can cultivate a distance from our thoughts. In short, we will practice attending to something *other* than our thoughts.

To aid us in investigating the nature of our thoughts, we will take a deep look at our conditioning. Conditioning is a term with which we also want to become familiar. By conditioning, I mean the ideas and concepts we grew up with and unconsciously incorporated into our belief system. These conditioned collections of thoughts and beliefs can be completely invisible to us when we first start—almost like a fish trying to become aware of the water in which it is swimming. But we will see that this "conditioning" forms a foundation of assumptions that directly affect our thinking and inform our identity. It's the basis for our "I like…," "I don't like…," "I am…" statements.

I recall being twenty years old and backpacking through Europe, wildly curious to see more of the world. I grew up near Seattle with a Dutch mother and an English father. My mom hated seafood (especially shellfish: clams, oysters, and mussels) and would give all kinds of descriptions about how awful it was, referring to the slimy texture and the sea brine taste, all of which were disgusting to her; thus, as a child I never ate it. Without even knowing it, I had unconsciously adopted an attitude that shellfish were gross. I would never sit down at a restaurant and order a steaming bowl of mussels. But when I was twenty, I found myself in the seaside resort of Arcachon, France. We were staying in the cheapest accommodations and had managed to score an attic room above a house/restaurant. I vividly recall coming to the dining area for dinner and noticing the patron's little boy (about three or four years old) eating at a nearby table. In front of him, he had a bowl of soup full of all kinds of shellfish, and he was eating it all with great gusto—slurping the mussels from their shells, picking up the fishy broth and drinking it, obviously enjoying every last morsel of his meal. At that moment, I had an epiphany. The little boy naturally loved shellfish, but I didn't actually know if I liked it or not because I had never tried it. I saw it, and my mind said "gross," and I moved on to ordering something else. I identified with *not liking* seafood—without ever having tried it! It's a small example, but a good one.

We usually define ourselves as a conglomeration of our likes and dislikes, what we think is right and wrong, what we perceive to be our strengths and weaknesses, etc. Maybe we were always picked last in gym class as a child and developed the thought "I am uncoordinated and bad at sports." From a child's point of view, that thought makes sense. Our classmates didn't pick us, so we must be bad at the sport, but that may or may not be accurate. Maybe we excel at a different type of sport. Perhaps peer pressure is involved. "I am uncoordinated and bad at sports" is just a thought. But that thought might inform many of our actions as we grow up.

As we embark on this journey, we begin to look at how much of who we think we are results from conditioned responses developed from habitual thinking. The thought (e.g., "I hate seafood" or "I am uncoordinated") has grown into an unexamined assumption. Without even knowing it, these uninvestigated thoughts can rule us. Often our beliefs cause us downright suffering. So, our new job is to begin investigating our thoughts. Eventually, we might rise to the bigger question: Without my conditioned thoughts as to right, wrong, good, and bad, *who am I*?

Don't worry. We'll take it slow.

Self-Inquiry

We will embark on a playful self-inquiry journey into the very heart of the matter. What do we *really* know to be true? What does our own experience show us?

When I started the self-inquiry journey, I didn't know what that meant. *What is self-inquiry?*

At the time, I took thinking for granted. As a college-educated person, I more or less ascribed to Descartes's philosophy "I think, therefore I am."

I had never stopped to investigate whether that was true. It seemed true. It felt true. Even better, it sounded brilliant. I didn't (perhaps couldn't) see it as a conditioned assumption; thus, it didn't occur to me to ask if I *must* be actively thinking to experience existence. Since thinking was an intrinsic part of my existence, I identified thinking as being "who I am."

True, I did sometimes experience peak thought-free moments of bliss, such as delighting in beauty, being overcome by love, or dancing with abandon. However, it still hadn't occurred to me that I could choose to identify with something other than my thinking mind.

It wasn't until I was smack dab in the middle of a mid-life crisis "suffer-fest" that I began to investigate how to lessen that suffering. What quickly came up was the notion that my thoughts themselves were tormenting me. Some of them were loud and obvious ("I am unlovable," "I failed," "I've been abandoned," "I am not enough"). Others were harder to pinpoint, like "Suffering is inevitable." (Is it?) Finally, I saw the need to distance myself from the thoughts eating me alive.

But to do that, I had to dive deeper. I had to practice noticing my thoughts arising and fading away—all on their own so that I could touch into the pure, alive beingness that exists *regardless of what the thinking mind is thinking.*

As practitioners delving into a journey of self-inquiry—a journey of getting naked in the now—contrary to popular belief, we must dive headlong into thoughts. We must investigate the very nature of thinking—especially our own thinking. We must develop the knack for witnessing our thoughts or cultivating what Ramana Maharshi calls "effortless awareness of being."

We start by becoming curious about the very process of thinking. What are all these thoughts that are happening? Can we notice them? Who is controlling them? Am I the master of the images and perceptions that come into my mind, or do they come unbidden? If I harbor a stressful belief, can I let it go? Why not? What is keeping me from letting it go? What is the nature of my thoughts? Are they positive thoughts? Negative? Commentary thoughts? What are they? Do my thoughts define me? Can I be free of my thoughts? Can I divert my attention? The journey into self-inquiry begins this way—with a willingness to start asking questions. Asking questions allows me to investigate the underlying assumptions I have lived by and watch the mind move with curiosity. The biggest question we will ultimately examine is this: Am I my thoughts?

Ready to dive into a self-inquiry practice?

The next series of practices will be little exercises to help you begin this journey of getting to know your mind—of befriending your thoughts, and by that, I mean becoming familiar with them. You don't have to like your thoughts; you only have to become familiar with them.

Earlier, we dove into a series of juicy practices that encouraged us to relax while directing our attention to a particular nurturing task. We started by kissing ourselves all over, allowing our attention to cascade down our bodies incrementally like a slow waterfall. Then, we practiced directing our attention to following the beloved's breath, first an external loved one and then ourselves. Afterward, we practiced moving all our attention to the senses, asking, what else is here (other than our thoughts)? Finally, we directed our attention smack dab into our heart center and relaxed and rested there, intentionally drawing our attention away from the head and mind and into the chest and heart. In each of these practices, we develop the knack of focusing on something other than our thoughts: body parts, the breath, senses, and the heart center.

Now, we are going to take a different approach. We are going to look directly at our thoughts. Instead of directing attention away from them, we will run to them—but with the eye of a child scientist, curious about what makes them tick.

To start, we will do a straightforward mindfulness exercise called Counting Your Thoughts. It is a practice that helps us recognize and accept we have thoughts and that they are just that: thoughts—a distinct phenomenon arising in consciousness, not unlike a visual or sound phenomenon—an observable thought phenomenon.

Don't overlook this exercise, even if you are an experienced meditator. It can be profoundly powerful to go back to fundamental practices. Over our journeys, we can develop a new kind of conditioning—"spiritual," which has its own overlay of beliefs and assumptions. We begin to feel like we know something. But becoming an awareness practitioner is not about becoming an expert in the subject; it is about being a perpetual beginner, facing each moment with fresh eyes. As Shunryu Suzuki, author of *Zen Mind Beginner's Mind*, says, "In the beginner's mind there are many possibilities, but in the expert's there are few."

Let's practice!

Practice #8: Counting and Accepting Your Thoughts

In this juicy practice, we are going to sit, as if in meditation, for just a few minutes, but with the very focused, simple goal of counting our thoughts. In this way, we have the opportunity to befriend our thinking mind—the beginning of developing a relationship with our perceptions, beliefs, and ideas.

Too often, we sit down to meditate and are bowled over by the many thoughts happening while we are supposed to be meditating. These thoughts might have to do with what we need to get done that day, or maybe they will be rehashing past conversations or worrying about the future. They are habitual, often predictable thoughts. It is a well-worn habit to think continuously. It is what our brain does. When we sit down to meditate, however, commonly, a secondary level of thoughts arises, judging our performance. The brain (always analyzing) points out all we are doing is thinking when what we are "supposed" to be doing is not thinking.

Today, we are not going to fight against the thinking mind at all. Instead, we will fully accept that we have thoughts. What we are going to do is pay close attention. For two minutes, we are simply going to count our thoughts.

As a thought comes to mind, we will accept it, count it, and let it float away.

"My back hurts"—one. "Oh yeah, I'm counting my thoughts"—two. "What are we having for dinner tonight?"—three. "Crap, did I leave the burner on?"—four. "I need to get up and check that"—five. "How long have I been doing this?"—six. "I really need to check the oven"—seven. "What time is it?"—eight.

Don't be surprised if your mind seems completely blank when you first turn your attention to counting your thoughts. Turning awareness on our thoughts can sometimes be like the effect of a deer in the headlights. Suddenly there is no movement at all—a kind of mental paralysis. But notice there is usually an associated thought with that observation: "I'm not thinking anything!"—one. "My mind is blank"—two.

I started this section by commenting on how I had unconsciously adopted Descartes's philosophy "I think, therefore I am," which meant my very identity was inextricably tied to thinking. Later, when I began a journey of self-inquiry, I swung the pendulum to the other side, trying to rid myself of thoughts as fast as possible.

Eventually, I came to appreciate neither of these is true. I cannot rid myself of thoughts, *and* I am not only my thoughts.

We are here to embark on a journey to discover that for ourselves, so let's start by accepting that we have thoughts and beginning to notice that they are not more important than the rest of our experiences. They are just thoughts, something we can observe, like our sensations, friends, and lovers.

I'll note that this is an easy exercise you can do several times during the day to break the habit of thinking by diving headlong into noticing thoughts directly and counting them. It is a powerful mindfulness practice.

The practice:

- Make sure you have a quiet, undistracted space and a timer handy, as well as a pen and paper.
- Start the timer for two minutes.
- Begin by closing your eyes and taking a breath through your nose, holding for one second, and then exhale completely. Repeat a few more times, then breathe normally for a few more breaths.
- Now, begin counting your thoughts. As one comes to mind, number it, accept it, and then let it float away.

- Notice that many thoughts are almost invisible "non-thoughts" like "I am not thinking anything" or "What am I doing again?" As soon as you notice them, count them. Don't worry about the nature of the content.
- Sometimes thoughts will come fast and furious. Don't stop and evaluate the content; keep counting as many as possible.
- When the alarm goes off, stop and make a note of how many thoughts you have had. The number doesn't matter. You are mindfully recognizing and noticing the process. The key is accepting that you have thoughts and that they are just that: thoughts.
- Take a moment to reflect on this exercise.

Notes: _____

_____

_____

_____

_____

_____

_____

_____

_____

Practice #9: Becoming a Thought Whisperer

As we've been discussing, there are different practices to help us investigate our thoughts on our journey to get naked in the now. So often, a thought stream captivates our attention such that we can't even see the individual phrases. As a result, we lose sight of everything else, consumed by what we are thinking.

Some of these practices, which we have begun to play with, encourage distancing from our thoughts. For example, we draw attention back to the senses, the breath, or a mantra to interrupt thinking. These are all helpful for stabilizing concentration.

Others, such as counting our thoughts, help us develop the capacity to witness our thinking mind — to step back and see that thoughts themselves are just a phenomenon that comes and goes.

As we continue our journey, we are encouraged to pay even closer attention to investigating the nature of thought. For example, can I watch and see if thoughts are always coming and going? *Can I watch an idea both arise in my consciousness and fade away?*

On my journey, this is what the teachers were encouraging me to practice. I've always found thoughts to be kind of clingy, however. So, the idea that a thought might fade away on its own or "self-liberate," as my teacher Joel Morwood puts it, seemed unlikely.

Thoughts have always felt like they belonged to me — like they *were* me. Plus, thoughts didn't seem to come in one at a time but more like a whole string, inextricably linked together — hence the term "train of thought." These thought streams seemed out of my control — more like a runaway train — and often nearly impossible to stop.

But as I embarked on my journey of self-inquiry, I kept practicing, curious to trust the process itself. After all, not only were my modern spiritual teachers (Joel Morwood, Cheri Huber, Adyashanti, Byron Katie, Eckhart Tolle, and others) telling me to look within, but also great mystics of the past (Rumi, Ibn Arabi, St. Teresa of Avila, Meister Eckhart, and many others) representing many religions (Hinduism, Islam, Buddhism, Christianity, Sufism, and Judaism). They were all saying the same thing: pay attention! Investigate the nature of thought. Watch it arise and fall away.

(If you are interested, by the way, in a great book that draws specifically from the wisdom of the mystics of all religions, I highly encourage you to read *Way of Selflessness: A Practical Guide to Enlightenment Based on the Teachings of the World's Great Mystics* by Joel Morwood.)

These modern and ancient teachers encourage practitioners to get deft enough in their examination to look between the thoughts—to investigate the gap between one thought and the next. And, they all agreed that the true nature of our being is something more than thoughts, opinions, memories, and personality—something that might be called Awareness, or the Source, or the underlying substrate of all, or God—something that reveals itself in that gap between thoughts.

But those sticky thoughts, especially the "I" ones such as "I am…" or "I don't like…," sure felt like me.

Gradually, during deep meditation, as happens on an extended silent retreat, I became more adept at watching my thoughts. I began to appreciate that there *were* gaps between the thoughts—though barely noticeable. And I discovered for myself that in those little gaps, there was a brightening and an expansion—a compelling momentary no-thought, in-breath of potential also marked by a sense of completeness and satisfaction—an alive, vibrant still point. *Is that where thoughts come from and where they go?*

I became curious about the "stickiness" of some of my thoughts so that I could rest in the gap more often.

I began to realize that when I went in to look at some thoughts, I was subconsciously reaffirming them. *Yep — there's that thought. It's real. It's mine. It's not going away.* Slowly, however, I realized that by checking in, I kept the thought from self-liberating, continually, though unconsciously, reifying it.

Have you ever heard a ringing gong and listened as the sound slowly faded to nothing? Well, with thoughts, it was as if every time I endeavored to watch that thought drift into nothing, I instead kept lightly hitting the thought gong — starting it up again, giving the impression it was all one perpetual and unstoppable thought train.

One day, while on a silent retreat, an unexpected image came to mind from a TV show called *Ghost Whisperer*. In the TV show, at the end of each episode, the main character, Melinda Gordon (played by Jennifer Love Hewitt), helps earthbound "stuck" (often persistent and menacing) spirits to cross over into the light. Melinda sees the ghosts for what they are — ephemeral spirits — and does not fear them, instead confidently guides them to leave this earthbound existence, to find their way into the light and back to the Source.

For whatever reason, a mental trick dawned on me. Perhaps, instead of using my brain to beat myself up for continually inadvertently re-pinging the sticky thoughts, I could imagine ushering those thoughts to liberation.

I could be a *Thought Whisperer*.

And this little trick is what I want to share with you.

When I started this practice, it helped my brain relax, and I think it might help you too. My brain liked the idea. It had a little job to do — which thankfully was no longer tied to endlessly investigating (and thus re-pinging) a particular thought — but rather to the compassionate, selfless act of ushering each sticky thought to liberation.

It sounds a bit cumbersome, but it quickly became joy-filled.

With each session during that retreat, I looked forward to noticing the thoughts that came.

There you are. I see you. Let's go into the light.

I imagined holding each in my upraised open palms and gently encouraging it to fly away. It was such a different experience—more relaxing, less tense.

More and more thoughts came during the sessions. I welcomed them all and offered each back to the Source. The meditation sessions became marked by the little brightening, expansive silent gaps I had noticed naturally occur between thoughts. With a little nudge from the Thought Whisperer, sticky convictions self-liberated, and as they did, awareness brightened.

As a Thought Whisperer, I no longer needed to fear that I would be held hostage by a particularly compelling one. Instead, I blessed each thought with my attention and sent it on its way.

One day, it dawned on me that the biggest question of all, "Who am I?"—the one that I had separated and put into a "how to get enlightened" category of its own—was no different from *any other thought.*

Shockingly, I suddenly saw that asking even the mother of all spiritual questions was not about finding an answer. Instead, it was another opportunity to release even that question to its Source.

From time to time, I still ask, when I am deep in meditation, "Who am I?"

But instead of looking for an answer, I let the Thought Whisperer invite me to fearlessly and selflessly usher that question and any related thoughts about it back to the Source.

For there—at the Source—is the peace and fulfillment I seek. And in it, there are no questions.

Before you ask, let me reassure you. You needn't spend weeks on silent meditation to do this practice; you can playfully engage today. This little trick is a shortcut to experiencing those clingy thoughts fade away.

It's best to stabilize attention first, allowing about twenty minutes of undistracted time to practice. So first, we will use one of our juicy practices to stabilize concentration, and then, when we are a bit settled, we will practice engaging our Thought Whisperer, ushering each thought into the light.

I appreciate that it can be hard to engage in practice while reading from a book. So, while I want to share the essence here, I also want to remind you that these practices are also available as guided awareness practices.

The practice:

- Begin by fully relaxing and bringing your attention to this moment. Then, like a lover approaching their beloved, preparing to offer a sensual massage, let's give all our attention to our body, kissing ourselves all over if you will.
- Let your body naturally relax for a moment.
- Now draw attention to the top of your head and feel as if it incrementally cascades down the head.
- The head tingles as the attention moves lower, coming to the eyes.
- Relax the eye sockets, feel the cascading warmth of attention now move to the cheeks, and allow the cheeks to drop.
- Now relax the mouth and allow the cascade to travel down the nape of your neck, down the shoulders.

- Drop the shoulders, feel attention sink lower, like gravity, going down each arm, finding its way to each finger, and coming into the chest.
- Relax the heart region. "You are safe. You are well. I love you," the attention seems to say as it passes through the heart.
- Allow the kisses to move down to the gut region. Unclench the gut, and allow the belly to soften.
- Kiss each hip with attention, and let it trickle between your legs, feeling a sweet tingling in what Eastern tradition calls the first or root chakra.
- Let it cascade around each thigh and find its way to your knees. Circle and love your knees with attention, for they often bear the brunt of carrying us.
- Allow attention to keep moving lower down the leg, relaxing the calf muscles, circling the ankles, and moving down through each toe into the ground.
- Sit for a moment in the delightful alive resonance of your attention, loving each part of your body.
- Bring your attention gently to the breath, simply noticing the rise and fall of the chest.
- Next, I am going to give you a series of instructions.
- To start, I'd like you to listen to the sound of a gong. (If you listen to my guided awareness practice, I will ring the gong. If you do this alone, you can find a gong sound on the internet. I like to use the Insight Timer app's "basu" gong.)
- Once the sound has started, I'd like you to follow the sound of the gong until it is completely gone. Then pay attention to what happens the moment the sound is entirely gone. We will mimic this effect but with our thoughts, adopting a trick when needed to help our thoughts fade away while we pay close attention.

- We'll generate a few thoughts intentionally to get us started. Generally, impersonal thoughts are less sticky, allowing us to practice watching a thought fade away.
- Think the thought "2 + 3 = 5." Then, allow it to fade away.
- Think the thought, "Trees are green." Then, allow it to fade away.
- Think the thought, "I am a writer." Allow it to fade away.
- Next, I'd like you to allow whatever thoughts want to arise naturally. Notice them as we have been doing, and then let them disappear, or "self-liberate" as my teacher Joel Morwood puts it.
- Practice this on your own for a while.
- Suppose you discover a thought that seems to be sticky and doesn't want to fade away, either generating a whole related thought stream or perpetually repeating itself. In that case, I want you to interrupt that tendency and be proactive as a Thought Whisperer.
- Picture the sticky thought lying on your upraised palm. Then, mentally raise your palm to the sky and offer it back to the source—like the Ghost Whisperer who helped spirits find their way back to the light.
- Be firm, kind, and encouraging to the sticky thought, acknowledging it but saying, "It's okay. You can go."
- Relax your body. Relax your mind. Rest in your chest region, allowing only a tiny piece of attention on the thought as it fades.
- Mentally, notice it getting lighter in your hand's palm, raising above the palm, while you murmur encouragement and stay centered.
- Look for the moment it disappears completely. What do you notice? Can you feel it fading? What happens when it is totally gone from your conscious mind?

- Repeat this process again and again with each thought you notice, training yourself to not only notice but encourage them to go.
- What was that practice like for you?

Notes: _____

_____

_____

_____

_____

_____

_____

_____

_____

Practice #10: Discovering Aliveness in Naked Feelings

On our self-discovery journey, we will investigate more than just our thoughts. We will tune in to our feelings as well. So let's become mad scientists exploring our feelings with microscopic care, searching for the purest experience—one that hasn't been hijacked by a thought first. But at first blush, we might find ourselves confused differentiating between thoughts, emotions, and feelings. I know I did.

Let me give you a quick example. Imagine you are riding a rickety roller coaster that has climbed up to its highest peak and is about to plummet down a steep and twisting path. Just as the cart begins the downslide, you might feel scared. Your heart might be racing, and you might feel butterflies in your stomach. Your brain might be internally shrieking, "Ahhhh! Not safe! How old is this thing anyway? Didn't I just read about someone getting thrown out of a roller coaster?"

In other words, we experience a mix of things: emotions (fear), physical sensations (racing heart), and thoughts ("Am I safe?"). Similarly, when you reach out and touch a hot stove, you "feel" the physical sensation of burning, accompanied quickly by feeling an emotion such as "fear" and perhaps having the thought "danger—get away."

As self-inquiry practitioners, we will learn to discern the difference, separating the physical sensations, emotions, and thoughts.

I think of it this way:

Thoughts are conscious ideas or opinions produced by thinking (verbal inner talk).

Emotions reflect subconscious responses to our environment (instinctive reaction).

Physical sensations are what happen in our body (physiological response).

But don't worry too much about this right now. I'm drawing your attention to it because we use the term "feel" in the English language rather indiscriminately. For instance, it's common to say, "I feel like I can't meditate." This sentence, however, does not express a feeling so much as a thought. A more accurate expression upon having trouble meditating would be to say something like, "I feel frustrated," defining the subconscious emotion rather than the surface thought. A more precise description would be to describe the actual sensations you are physically feeling. "I feel my brow furrowed and my eyes are squinting."

The reason we want to become adept at this discernment process is primal and supremely important. Growing up, we learn to label things quickly—a habit that draws us away from what is physically happening in the body and puts us in our heads, imagining and telling stories about what it means. This tendency often leads us to avoid specific experiences, fearing our reaction or inappropriate response.

There is a classic Zen story illustrating this effect. You are walking on a trail and suddenly see a snake across the path. Your heart begins beating wildly and your eyes widen as your head screams, "Snake!" You jump back, quivering. A moment later, you realize the "snake" is just a stick.

We hear even more dramatic but similar stories from those with post-traumatic stress disorder (PTSD). In PTSD, this response system of assigning thoughts and emotions to physical sensations is exacerbated, becoming chronic and debilitating, invoking the fight or flight response for no reason.

We live on the outskirts of Las Vegas in Calico Basin, next to Red Rock Canyon National Conservation Area (200,000 acres of geological wonder in the Mohave Desert known for its iconic red sandstone cliffs). Calico Basin is just twenty minutes east of the Las Vegas strip but about as different from and unique as the casino-laden street. In the house we recently moved into, a prior resident was a firefighter who suffered quietly from PTSD. Certain loud sounds, such as might have been heard during a traumatic fire, including machinery and loudspeakers, triggered him. However, those sounds had nothing to do with what was happening. At the instance of sound, his body reacted physically, causing his heart to race and his face to flush. These physical sensations, in turn, were associated with the need to take aggressive action—to save the baby from the burning house.

At one point, tour helicopters took to hovering over his house, blaring through loudspeakers about the history and geology of the nearby sandstone cliffs. These sounds and resulting physical sensations induced an aggressive and severe fight response. His brain told him that these sounds meant immediate danger requiring his action. One day he became unhinged, grabbed a BB gun, and began firing upon the helicopter. In the end, he didn't hurt anybody, but his extreme reaction was the impetus for moving away from the beloved home he had remodeled.

We may not all suffer from debilitating PTSD, but we all habitually confuse our physical sensations with our thoughts and emotions about those sensations. As awareness practitioners, we want to realize that thoughts, emotions, and bodily sensations are all disparate things that we tend to lump together, causing us undue suffering.

Instead, we want to practice feeling the purely physical sensations, isolated from the emotions and thoughts about those bodily feelings so we can fully experience them in their naked form.

Why is that? Because, at the center of all afflicted emotions— the mystics tell us—is pure wisdom energy: the naked feeling of being fully alive, marked by alert clarity, loving compassion, peaceful ease, natural wisdom, and spacious stillness.

Society teaches us that certain emotions are "bad," such as fear, anger, and envy. But when we dig a little deeper, we discover the feeling itself is not the problem. Instead, it is our positive or negative reaction that is the problem.

Remember that roller coaster ride, the physical sensations — racing heart, butterflies in the stomach? Those are the same physical sensations as excitement but with different thoughts attached. The mystics teach us that learning to isolate the physical phenomena from the ideas and beliefs about those sensations helps us transform the afflicted emotion and experience the wisdom energy instead.

Mystics are not the only ones who recognize the importance of this lesson; it is also well-known as a psychology tool. And it is counterintuitive to our instincts. When a strong emotion arises, we tend to want that emotion to go away. We habitually dislike certain bodily sensations that have become associated with strong feelings and can even be afraid of them. In other words, we believe our thoughts about physical sensations. So, for instance, a racing heart becomes associated only with danger—not with something fun and exciting about to happen or with getting stronger by challenging my heart to beat faster once in a while.

Psychologists and mystics say that the better course is to dive right in instead of running away from these feelings. For example, when a feeling has become overwhelmingly negative, it's time to look at the thoughts associated with the physical sensation and then practice experiencing those sensations without the thoughts attached.

Psychologists call this the cognitive behavioral therapy technique, or "brain re-training." One, in particular, is called interoceptive exposure, which essentially means becoming aware of the body's physical sensations by intentionally exposing yourself to them and paying attention to the actual physiological experience instead of the thoughts about it. So, if you want to create a racing heart intentionally, you might run in place for a minute. Or, if you have come to associate body tingling with the fear of disease, you can practice hyperventilating to induce a tingling sensation intentionally.

Another way to do this is simply by thinking about a situation that brings you some form of stress. Reimagining a scenario can re-create physical sensations as well. So, if you fear heights, imagining yourself on the edge of a skyscraper roof, looking down, might bring up the classic fear responses of sweaty palms and a beating heart. In the movie *Free Solo*, about rock climber Alex Honnold scaling the three-thousand-foot granite walls of El Capitan without ropes, audience members the world around reported getting sweaty palms just from watching the movie.

When you recall an incident to bring up the physical sensations, the trick is to let the story (i.e., thoughts and emotions) go entirely. You know you are not actually on the top of a building, for instance. So instead, the training is to pay minute attention to the physical sensations themselves, apart from the story.

Physical sensations themselves are not a problem. They just are. Sweaty palms do not mean that danger is present; they are just sweaty palms. You begin to notice that physiological sensations are not themselves catastrophic. You begin to separate the suffering story from the feeling. You begin to stop taking physical sensations personally, and instead get curious about them.

What happens next is like the gap between the thoughts we discussed: there can be an opening for pure awareness to reveal itself. Earlier I called this the naked feeling of being fully alive, marked by alert clarity, loving compassion, peaceful ease, natural wisdom, and spacious stillness. This naked feeling of pure awareness might feel like tingling all over. Or, it might feel exciting, and your heart could even be racing.

Being without our stories can initially seem disorienting, but that bewilderment holds the highest wisdom energy of all: Gnosis—perfect knowledge of spiritual mysteries.

Are you intrigued? Is your mad scientist chomping at the bit, just a little, curious if you, too, might rest in the naked feeling of pulsing aliveness?

Thoughts vs. Emotions vs. Sensations

Let's start this way. Let's take a quick look at the broad strokes of thoughts versus emotions versus sensations, just to be sure we are on the same page.

Below is a list of statements. Please read them to yourself and notice which ones are thoughts, which are emotions, and which are physical feelings. Remember, we use the word "feel" for all these experiences. Sometimes the word feel is associated with a surface thought about things; sometimes, it refers to emotion (i.e., deep-rooted, often unconscious instincts about things); and sometimes, we use it to reference a physical sensation (what the body feels). Can you see the difference?

Self

I feel like I am not worthy. (thought)
I feel ashamed. (emotion)
My face feels hot. (physical sensation)

Relationships

I feel like you don't like me. (thought)
I feel sad. (emotion)
I feel a heavy sensation in my chest. (physical sensation)

I feel like you purposefully antagonize me. (thought)
I feel mad. (emotion)

I feel my eyes narrowing and my nostrils flaring. (physical sensation)

Life

I feel overwhelmed by life. (thought)

I feel confused. (emotion)

I feel dizzy. (physical sensation)

Health

I feel sick. (thought)

I feel scared of dying. (emotion)

I feel a heaviness in my body. (physical sensation)

Roller coaster example

I feel like my life might be in danger. (thought)

I feel scared. (emotion)

I feel my heart racing. (physical sensation)

Firefighter example

I feel like something terrible is happening and I must act. (thought)

I feel terrified. (emotion)

I feel my heart racing, and I am squinting my eyes. (physical sensation)

These are just a few examples to help us remember to distinguish between a thought, an emotion, and a physical sensation. We do this to discourage the habitual labeling and storytelling in our heads that makes us think something is wrong. We do this so that we can practice letting go of the thoughts and emotions which are causing us suffering. When we are suffering, our world view is narrow, painful, and constricted.

Suffering keeps us from experiencing the present moment because suffering is tied to a story in the head saying over and over again some version of "poor me." It enhances an ego-I identity. On the other hand, when we are not suffering, we are open, lit up, energetic, clear, and at ease.

If we pay attention, there is a loss of ownership of the moment. We experience physical sensations as they are happening but with a little detachment. When we do, we lose our overt self-consciousness and delight in fully being with what's unfolding. The world is happening, and we are participating, but we are not perpetually self-referencing. A butterfly lands on our hand, and we spontaneously feel enlivened and energized for a moment. The sun sets, leaving a dashing pink-striped sky, and we experience a little in-breath of joy. Even a pounding headache can become a curiosity about the minute sensations as we pay close attention instead of a cause for worry. A good friend once said that her highest mystical experience came when she suffered from the worst back pain in her life—an "11 out of 10," she said. During the worst of it, she could not think about her situation and could only sit there from moment to moment, noticing the physical feelings as they rose and passed away in quick succession. Her experience? Bliss.

Even though the potential is excellent, please take care not to overwhelm yourself in the following two practices. First, start with small, easy examples that are not likely to trigger a strong emotion. This way, you can practice isolating physical sensations from thoughts and feelings in baby steps. Later, if you want to dive into stronger emotions but are prone to PTSD or panic attacks, it is helpful to have support—someone to remind you that whatever it is you are feeling is not happening now. The brain is a powerfully conditioned machine. We can retrain our brain, but we need to start slowly—as when you start jogging, you don't start by running a marathon. Instead, you train first, building up muscle.

Recreating a physical sensation

In this example, we will recreate a physical sensation typically associated with a series of thoughts and emotions, fully aware that there is no background story, and allow ourselves to focus only on the physical sensations themselves.

Below is a list of physical activities that can mimic an emotional response. (These have been adapted from the Beck Institute of Cognitive Behavior Therapy.)

- Dizziness, headache: shake head side to side quickly for 30 seconds with eyes open
- A tight throat, breathless or dry mouth: swallow quickly ten times
- Chest tightness, breathlessness, hot flashes: breathe as deeply as possible using a straw for 30 seconds
- Disorientation, nausea: place your head between legs for 30 seconds
- Heart racing, feelings of heat: run in place for 60 seconds
- Lightheadedness: hold your breath for 60 seconds
- Dizziness: spin for 30 seconds

The practice (two techniques):

Technique 1: mimicking the sensation

- Pick which sensation causes you the most trouble and is usually associated with suffering thoughts. For example, maybe you have a health anxiety symptom that compels you to worry, so whenever you feel a lump in your throat, your first thought is, "Do I have throat cancer?" Or maybe when someone says something in a particular tone, you find your heart racing, and immediately the thought comes that you are in mortal danger.

- Next, intentionally practice the activity that will mimic the physical sensation (see list above).
- When the physical sensation becomes intolerable, investigate your experience. Ask yourself:
  - What am I worried will happen?
  - Was it as bad as I expected?
  - What would happen if I kept going?
  - What did I learn?
- Questioning is the first step in desensitizing yourself so that you are freer to stop and feel physical sensations as they arise without being bombarded with terrifying imagined thoughts about what is happening.
- Pay attention to the feeling of uncertainty in beginning the exercise and intentionally going to an uncomfortable place.
- Notice your willingness to experience the previously terrifying sensations and acknowledge the courage and strength it took to do that without employing an avoidance strategy or safety behavior. On this journey of self-discovery and transformation, it is good to offer ourselves encouragement and support. This is challenging work!

Notes: _____

_____

_____

_____

_____

_____

_____

_____

_____

Technique 2: Using our imagination to recreate a scene

- Remember to start with something easy—not your worst memory or most traumatic experience.
- Get yourself settled into a comfortable position.
- Stabilize your attention by following your breath or practicing prayer in the heart for five or ten minutes. No rush; be at ease with yourself.
- Now intentionally bring up a painful story from your past. Allow yourself to get upset thinking about it. Notice the thoughts about this old injury. Maybe something like "So and so betrayed me," or "I deserved the promotion more than so and so." There will likely be some emotions, too, such as sadness, anger, or jealousy. In addition, if you have successfully brought up the old injury in your mind's eye, there will probably even be physical sensations. Maybe your stomach hurts, your shoulders slump, your chest caves in, or your heart races.
- Next, deliberately allow the thoughts and emotions about the incident to float away. Practice being the Thought Whisperer, if it helps, and let them go.
- Notice only the remaining physical sensations.
- Use your brain to describe to yourself what the physical sensations are in minute detail. Get creative, use metaphor, but focus only on the physical sensations. "My chest feels heavy and dense like an overripe banana." "My head tingles like a thousand fairies dancing inside." "My breathing is constricted as if a 200-pound sumo wrestler is sitting on me."
- Rest. Breathe. Sit still.
- Watch as the significant physical sensations dissipate on their own when we direct attention away from the story

about what is happening—like a gong sound slowly fading.

- Now, allow your attention to spread in all directions into the all-encompassing space. Feel a hint of a smile gently pulsing behind your cheeks as if you have just turned your face to the sunlight.
- Warmth spreading. No boundaries. Open. Attentive to all.
- You are pulsing with aliveness.
- Take a moment to write about what the experience was like, what you noticed.

Notes: _____

_____

_____

_____

_____

_____

_____

_____

_____

Chapter 6

Inner Striptease
(Letting Go of Who You Think You Are)

In order to swim, one takes off all one's clothes —
in order to aspire to the truth,
one must undress in a far more inward sense,
divest oneself of all one's inward clothes —
of thoughts, conceptions, selfishness, etc.
before one is sufficiently naked.
    —Soren Kierkegaard

When you strip without being ashamed,
and you take your clothes
and put them under your feet
like little children and trample them,
then you will see the son of the living one
and you will not be afraid.
    —Gospel of Thomas

When we started on this journey together, I talked about why I use the term "naked" in the title and why it features so prominently in this book. I spoke of wanting to intentionally invoke both the conditioned response that being naked tends to invoke: vulnerability, exposure, judgment, shame, and fear, but also wanting to point to the juiciness that being naked inspires, including innocence, playfulness, intimacy, passion, and love.

This book is about stripping ourselves of thinking of nakedness as something shameful and fearful and instead embracing being naked as a metaphor for feeling juicy and alive with pure potential unfolding. It's about digging deep below our thoughts and emotions, letting go of who we think we are to encounter what is left. Essentially, it is about embarking on an inner striptease that reveals to us the difference between being naked and naked being.

In either case, we might feel small before something mightier than our ego self, but the difference is significant. When we feel exposed and shamed, we fear being naked before unseen powerful forces out to harm us. But conversely, when we feel awash in love, enriched, and humbled before forces more fantastic than our small ego, we bask in the glory of our naked being.

In this chapter, we will begin our inner striptease. We have some territory to cover as we explore how we go about feeling awash in love.

First, we will practice identifying what it feels like to be in a state of naked reverence, humbled before forces that are vaster than our small ego.

Then, we will dare to take off our armoring of "knowledge" and instead tap into our inner wisdom and dapple in the esoteric arts of divination as we awaken the slumber of our subconscious mind. I call this letting guidance in.

Next, we will examine our beliefs about ourselves, intentionally get out of our comfort zone, and learn the power of asking ourselves, when confronted with a particularly limiting belief, "Is that so?"

Following that, we will go further into the murky depths of what we think we know as we examine the boundaries we believe exist between us and the world and what we think we know to be true about ourselves. Finally, we will investigate through our direct experience the power of attention and the experience of naked awareness.

Come with me as we begin our inner striptease.

Practice #11: Naked Reverence

So how do we move our perspective from one of fear to one of love? How do we strip ourselves of everything and be not in fear of being naked but full of potential for touching into our naked being?

For me, it was about accessing a state of naked reverence — a humbling letting go of my demands for perfection in myself constantly shaming me. I saw the hubris of my ways — that the coverings of my conditioning kept me from seeing myself as beautiful. Instead, my inner thoughts perpetually reminded me that I was an imperfect version of life: not thin enough, not smart enough, not rich enough, not spiritual enough, not successful enough, not young enough, not beautiful enough.

But beauty, like truth, can't help but shine when seen through an internal version of speaking truth to power (to borrow a political phrase). The power I am up against on any given day is the power of conditioning; the truth I need to speak to is a relaxed, silent acceptance of myself exactly as I am.

Not that I can't change, but that I can let go of the belief that fear and shame are what propel that change.

This inner speaking of truth to power began for me at a clothing-optional hot springs resort called Harbin Hot Springs. In an environment where almost all present were physically naked, I faced my deepest (mature-woman) body-shame fears and encountered the difference between being naked and naked being.

I stood near the pool's edge, wrapped in a sarong, that day. The thoughts clamoring in my head shamed me about my puffy belly, non-pert breasts, wrinkled eyes, and drooping butt. I felt shy and less than perfect.

After a long moment's hesitation — self-conscious that I wasn't thirty-five or even forty-five anymore — I finally stepped out of my sarong; not so much as a fig leaf was covering me. I moved through the grounds toward the warm pool and felt myself inexplicably relaxing. Despite my nakedness, I realized I didn't feel exposed and judged by others so much as protected and accepted.

I didn't expect that.

Maybe, I took metaphorical comfort in the fact there was an enormous fig tree offering all of us present its modest protection. The majestic fig tree reigned supreme over the grounds with extensive branches hanging over the warm pool, shading the people taking shelter under it and framing the sign that requested participants to refrain from conversation and sexual activity.

I had arrived at Harbin Hot Springs—a clothing-optional resort known for hosting all kinds of meditation, relationship, massage, and yoga retreats—located not far from Napa Valley.

I stepped into the large, warm pool, which at four and a half feet deep came up to my neck and, at a temperature of 95 to 98 (essentially body temperature) degrees, enveloped me like a womb. There were probably twenty or more other people in the pool. It was a mixed group: singles, couples—both same-sex and not—black, white, brown, and ranging in age from twenty to eighty. All were resting quietly, reverently, in the warm water under the arms of the giant fig tree. When I stopped and noticed, I realized that the people's energy was sweet, without aggressive overtones and uncomfortable overtures: just people gathering in meditative silence, collectively enjoying the sensation of warm water against their skin.

I relaxed and silently took in my surroundings. At one end, a middle-aged gay couple held hands, and along the long edge, a young tattooed and pierced woman lay horizontal atop the water, feet resting on a bar for support. In the center, a sixty-something woman cradled her partner in the center of the pool using the practice of Watsu—a form of aquatic bodywork used for deep relaxation. It was impossible not to notice the compassion and love reflecting off her face as she gently moved his body in sweeping arcs through the water.

My husband offered to do a Watsu session on me. As he supported and floated me in the warm water, I could not keep the joy from spreading across my face; such was the delight.

Scores of naked people entered and left quietly: up and down the stairs to the warm pool, or into the sanctuary of the hot pool (114 degrees), and then on up to the cold plunge (65 degrees)—a heavenly experience. I appreciated that no one looked like the cover of a checkout-stand magazine. I saw breasts and bottoms, bellies and genitals of every conceivable shape and size. Nobody was "perfect" by some coveted Hollywood ideal, yet each was undeniably beautiful and perfectly unique.

Sitting in the protected warmth surrounded by a diverse sampling of humanity, it was easy to turn attention away from the chatter of years of conditioned judgment and comparison, years of shame, and instead, just be. Still. Warm. Loved. Accepted. Beautiful exactly as I am.

Perhaps experiencing oneself and others—even life itself—as eternally beautiful, as intrinsically ecstatic, I mused, depends not so much on a particular set of attributes, per se, but on a state of naked reverence. For it seemed, in that "au natural" state of being, without the covering of conditioning, beauty, like truth—can't help but shine through, irrespective of size, shape, color, or particular leanings.

That moment at Harbin Hot Springs humbled me. Finally, I chose not to listen to the thoughts that usually ruled my head. So instead, I basked in the glory of the warm water on my skin, appreciated the silent companionship of fellow hot springers, and accepted that my unique appearance was as beautiful and worthy as anybody else's.

What should I listen to? I wondered. The inner voice that tells me I am not good enough? Or the sound of the wind gently rustling through an enormous fig tree? Should I focus on how to improve my appearance, or relax and feel the warm water on my skin? Who says breasts should be pert? Who says wrinkles are bad? Who judges me so? Not these gentle folk lost in their own reverie. Not the fig tree standing sentinel or the mulberry tree bursting with ripe fruit. Not the babbling natural springs bringing me joy. Not the sky, whose ubiquitous presence never minded the days when clouds threatened.

Years later, Harbin Hot Springs burned down during the Great Valley Fire of 2015. Cleaning up and moving forward—of rebuilding the sacred space—was expected to take some time. During that time, the community sent out a message:

> Imagine how you might "introduce a little Harbin" into your life on a regular basis. A daily walk in nature? An inspirational altar where you meditate? An unconditional dance in your living room? A moment to journal your gratitude? A leisurely meal with friends or family? A quiet soak in your tub before a good night's sleep?

The words reminded me of the impact that my awakening to my own perfection had, for even amidst destruction and devastation, cultivating a Harbin attitude of acceptance—what I might call a little Naked Reverence—can open the doorway to ecstatic living in all its happy, sad, perfect, and imperfect glory.

Today, I invite you to cultivate some of that Naked Reverence into your day.

The practice:

- Set some quiet time aside for this exercise. Imagine, if you will, that this is a date with yourself. You are planning to arrive naked and open, vulnerable, anticipating and hopeful that your own arms of acceptance will invite you in. As you prepare for your date, allow the feeling of excitement to creep in. You know this person; this person has such potential. This person is a good, sweet person, longing for connection.

- Draw a warm bath for yourself, or set aside some intentional time for a luxuriously long shower if you don't have a bathtub available.

- Imagine that this particular bath or shower is a sacred ritual in which you are going to speak truth to power. You will silently talk through the voice of silence and loving acceptance to the conditioned inner voices habitually shaming you.

- You will stand before that warm water and drop your clothes, intentionally stepping into the hot water and focusing all your attention on the affection you feel from the water caressing you, enveloping you, accepting you.

- Allow the reverent silence of your inherent perfection to grow and expand. Feel your intrinsic worth, the unique beauty of your being, and the total and utter acceptance by the water.

- Allow yourself to see yourself in your mind's eye, a gentle smile crossing your face as you receive the gift of acceptance and protection. This silent loving embrace that humbles those voices of shame is you—a vast and unconditional love that is your deepest self.

- Align yourself with the naked juicy potential this acceptance invites. If there were nothing wrong with you, what might be possible?

- Notice how the cheeks want to smile, how the skin begins to tingle.

- Allow that state of naked reverence to engulf you, something much bigger than the shaming voices.
- This is Naked Reverence.
- What did you notice?

Notes: _____

_____

_____

_____

_____

_____

_____

_____

_____

_____

Practice #12: Letting Guidance In — Consulting Ancient Divination Tools

Things that make you go hmm...
— C+C Music Factory

I value those who are considered "experts" in their field. I trust the scientists who have studied how viruses spread, for instance, or those who grow fuel from algae. I love researching and learning new things, have always been an A student, and want to excel at knowing stuff.

I love learning and developing expertise myself. I used to love going into university libraries where I had access to so much knowledge. With the advent of smartphones, I have never worried about too much screen time spent online. Instead, I quietly love that the iPhone gives me perpetual access to the internet. To me, it's like carrying the world's most extensive library with me in my pocket. So cool.

In social settings, I am always quick to look up answers. I can barely stand to allow a question to sit unanswered for more than five minutes before my phone is out, and I offer to look up the answer online. My phone research might vary from "Who is the lead actor in xxx movie?" to "What is the best way to heal a Jones fracture of the fifth metatarsal?"

I trust myself to research carefully — to investigate something from several angles, to read and consider both sides of an issue. And honestly, I enjoy adopting an attitude of knowingness on the subject. I appreciate feeling confident, strong, and in control.

But below the surface of societal interactions, I have realized that, to uncover naked awareness, I must drop the girding of knowledge that holds the mystery of life at bay. I must be willing to sit in the mystery of life, unprotected by expertise. I must be keen for the answers to reveal themselves organically — to allow the ways of the universe to guide me.

It's hard to say what this entails. But it feels like surrendering, if you will—to the possibility of something grander and more mysterious than our finite book knowledge.

Mystics have hinted at this kind of inner guidance for thousands of years. It is the kind of subconscious guidance we might receive from dreams, or forms of esoteric divination, such as the *I Ching*. And it is with what we connect when we notice synchronicities in our life. The modern saying "things that make you go hmmm" captures it well. But unfortunately, our logical, rational, educated minds can make no sense of subconscious guidance. Where is the science? Who is the expert?

To enter the mystery of life, however, we must let go of expecting a definitive answer and open ourselves to the possibility of gaining insight into the question and ourselves instead. We must practice tapping into our subconscious, trusting our intuition, and learning to see the patterns and themes of our lives without our biases (scientific or otherwise).

Maybe this sounds like a lot to take for granted.

But consider this: we subconsciously know that life is full of mystery that cannot be fully explained by what we think we know at any given moment. Even scientific knowledge morphs with the times: "The earth is flat" versus "The earth is round"; "Low-fat food is best for you" versus "High-fat food is best for you."

Still, we have trouble trusting a "greater than our thinking minds" innate wisdom to guide us. Should I trust the mystery to reveal itself? That feels like tricky territory. Where do I even start?

For me, I started with tarot cards. And before you form an opinion about tarot cards, let me tell you a story.

I grew up in a non-religious, science-based, loving family. Growing up, my dad was an engineer/skeptic who preferred to live life on the surface—not one for deep conversations. My mom was always a nurturing, kind soul who actively pursued alternative health; my brother loved animals and the great outdoors. I was a driven, straight-A-type student, somewhat innocent of the ways of the world.

My life had proceeded normally enough. I went to college, met my husband-to-be, got married, had kids, and often felt happy, except for the nagging feeling that the other shoe was going to drop. And sure enough, it did.

When I was thirty-three years old, I found myself smack dab in the middle of a mid-life crisis spurred by my husband having an affair with my best friend. The event triggered flashbacks of childhood sexual trauma of which I had no prior memory.

All of a sudden, I wasn't sure about anything in life. I wasn't sure if I could trust my husband. I wasn't sure if I could trust these new memories, and I didn't know where to turn. I was on shaky ground. The juicy details of that journey are the subject of my memoir, so I won't delve into them here. But suffice it to say, the events were a catalyst to beginning a spiritual journey of unlearning what I thought I knew. It was a journey that also upended what I thought about how to learn.

My husband and I started by seeking a therapist's help and then embarked on something new. We decided to take a yearlong love and ecstasy training that promised to rekindle intimacy. We agreed to attend three ten-day retreats and weekend gatherings in between. We were to spend time in meditation, time playing and dancing, and time in group sessions working together.

It was all new to us. We had never perused the "self-help," "religious," "spiritual," or "New Age" shelves of bookstores and libraries. My husband had read Carlos Castaneda, but I hadn't even gotten that far.

These workshops were a grand leap into the unknown. Still, we were motivated to try something different and new that would shatter our old ways of thinking and reopen the door for a fresh start.

I hadn't anticipated how it would look.

Some of the things that happened soon after we started were some fascinating coincidences. At first, I felt confident thinking of them as mere coincidences. But they began to pile up and became more astounding; I began to see them more as messages from the universe, or divine winks.

One of the first things that happened to me occurred in the morning meditation during the first ten-day session of our yearlong training. Although we were not experienced meditators and still felt ill-prepared to sit for long stretches, we were gung ho, committed to participating in every part of the retreat. So, we always went to the morning yoga and meditation. We found it easy to sit quietly in a large group of people who were also sitting quietly.

By and by, I began to have strange images spontaneously appear during these morning meditations. An experienced meditator might have ignored the visions, seeking, instead, a pure mind. But I was inexperienced and had never seen a "vision" before. I didn't understand what was happening and was curious about them. In one, a knight was bearing a large sword on a horse galloping hard. In another, a large heart sat amidst a violent storm pierced through with three blades. What did it mean?

One day, during a break, I decided to describe to a small group of participants the strange pictures that came to my mind during meditation. One girl turned toward me and told me I was describing different tarot cards. Then, she showed me cards from her set. I was stunned. What? No way.

I had never seen traditional tarot cards before. I don't recall all the cards I described, but I remember one of them was the Three of Swords, and another was the Knight of Swords. I was fascinated that my mind could come up with pictures found on cards that I had never seen before. Even more fascinating was what these cards represented.

The Knight of Swords (pictured as a charging knight on horseback with a raised sword) symbolizes charging forward with significant momentum and little regard for the dangers one may encounter. It is a card of fearlessness and invincibility.

The Three of Swords (pictured as a heart with three swords piercing it amid a terrible storm) is about abandonment, betrayal, and extreme pain. But when it shows up in a reading, it indicates an opportunity to expand and learn and the ability to conquer any pain that comes your way.

I began having other visions, too; some were prophetic, foreshadowing some unusual scene that would show up in my life some days later.

I felt like Dorothy in the land of Oz—no longer in Kansas.

The tarot's symbolic meanings of my visions, described to me, helped me immeasurably. They put words to what was brewing inside, but I couldn't quite see. When I tuned in, I felt myself to be that knight charging into danger somewhat recklessly but bravely too. Was it a good idea to study sexuality and intimacy in a group setting with a partner who had just been unfaithful? I wondered. But I couldn't erase a more profound sense that charging into the mess wholeheartedly, instead of ignoring and burying the pain, was the best path forward to a stronger love connection.

The tarot card symbolism also allowed me to paint a positive picture of the future. I felt incapacitated by the unbearable pain of betrayal and abandonment. I was deeply encouraged that the tarot card symbol came with the suggestion that I could bear that pain and grow from it. "I will be vulnerable amid pain and grow stronger from it" became a silent mantra.

As I experienced these mind-blowing divine winks from the universe, I realized that something more significant than my small self was available to help. I saw I could tap into my subconscious as well as a stream of unconscious wisdom that spoke in symbols. I didn't intellectually need to understand what it was or how it worked. All it required was to let go or, at least, temporarily suspend my ideas about how I thought the world worked and what I thought I knew.

Because of the synchronicity of my crazy tarot card visions, I became interested in esoteric divination for the first time in my life. I began studying the tarot, particularly the Osho Zen Tarot, and delving into the *I Ching*—one of the oldest of all classical divination systems, over three thousand years old. This course of study is not surprising, perhaps. Some say consulting the *I Ching* and the tarot works by synchronicity or meaningful coincidence (to borrow Jung's term). Jung reportedly said the *I Ching* or tarot were helpful ways to tap into the subconscious, similar to dream interpretation.

The two are a bit different. The *I Ching* helps us find patterns amid chaos, while tarot cards use images to prompt intuition. Either way, the goal is to promote self-empowerment by bringing the subconscious into the light of day.

Both require the participant to admit that they "don't know" how to move forward. To query a divination tool, one must tune in to their own burning questions and do what is often difficult—to ask for help.

Under any circumstances, it is humbling to ask for help, for we risk not being in control. When querying tarot cards or the *I Ching*, we tend to face some of our biggest questions in life. And we tend to be fully aware that our go-to, conditioned way of dealing with a situation has not helped. Plus, the "who" from whom we are asking for help is not a renowned scientist but the unseen mystery of the universe at large.

One of the best uses of these tools is not that they help us predict the future so much as help us reimagine and create new and unexpected possibilities. Sitting down before tarot cards or the *I Ching* is a way of stripping away our old way of being and responding and opening to a new way of seeing. We learn to be open, listen carefully, become attuned to resonance, and surrender what we think we know.

I highly encourage you to play with tarot cards or the *I Ching*. You can practice these methods on your own or with a practitioner. I think both are valuable. I spent years studying both of these on my own. Some books make it easy. Learning on your own has the advantage of convenience; there is no financial or scheduling barrier to cross each time you want to consult them. I loved diving into the allegorical symbolism of the cards and the organizing principles or what has been called the "philosophical taxonomy" of the *I Ching*. We humans are unique, and yet we face many of the same iconic struggles.

So, what happens when we consult a divination tool? We use the tool as a vehicle to expose what we already know but are unable or unwilling to recognize. Using a divination tool allows us to have a detached perspective—to open a window to our naked soul.

Consulting the tarot

A traditional tarot deck is comprised of seventy-eight cards divided into two groups: the major arcana (twenty-two cards) and the minor arcana (fifty-six cards). The major arcana cards represent the structure of human consciousness. They include classic life lessons, karmic influences, and big archetypal themes that can influence your life and journey. When these show up in a reading, pay attention! The minor arcana cards, divided into four groups or suits, tend to relate to what's happening in your daily life and have a more temporary influence.

The four suits are Cups (representing feelings, emotions, creativity), Pentacles (finances, work, possessions), Swords (thoughts, words, actions), and Wands (energy, motivation, passion). Each suit has ten numbered cards and four court cards. The four court cards represent different personality characteristics.

The most traditional deck out there is probably the Rider-Waite deck. I have used this deck quite a bit. This deck reflects those pictures that showed up in my vision. The deck I use the most, however, is the Osho Zen Tarot deck. I find the pictures to be beautiful and mesmerizing. It's a slightly different system, focused on understanding the here and now rather than predicting the future. The wisdom of Zen—the basis for these cards—says events in the outer world reflect our thoughts and feelings even when we are unclear. The Osho Zen Tarot deck is divided similarly to a traditional deck but with different word choices and, thus, a different focus. The suits are Water (cups), Rainbows (pentacles), Clouds (swords), and Fire (wands). There is one extra "Master" card. The Osho Zen Tarot deck is still my preferred go-to deck.

I have many stories from this deck, which I have owned since 1996. Once, around 2012 when I was having a tough time as I approached menopause, I lost one of the cards from the deck. Fittingly, it was the Courage card. Eighteen months later, just after a personal transformation that culminated in publishing my first book, I found the card half buried under the apple tree in my yard. So, I have a close connection to these cards.

Note: While writing this very chapter, I decided to consult my Osho Zen Tarot cards and do a reading about this book. I did a five-card layout with the central issue in the middle and four cards around it. I gasped as the reading unfolded. (See Appendix B for the details of the reading.)

The practice:

- The first task is in selecting a deck to work with.
- Elena Nicolaou, a culture editor at OprahMag.com, says, "There is no one correct deck. Look for the one that will literally speak to you."
- Find your question.
- Sit quietly and ponder your present issue until you have clarity about what you would like to query.
- Select a layout.
- Usually, the book that comes with the cards will have some suggestions. These range from a one-card draw to a ten-card layout. I almost always do a five-card layout with the Osho Zen Tarot cards which offers an overview of the issue. Whereas with the Rider-Waite deck, I often do a three-card (past, present, future) format.
- Shuffle the cards.
- Imagine that the cards are a receptacle into which you pour your energy.
- Fan the cards out using your left hand, which is said to be the receptive hand.
- Carefully choose the number of cards your layout requires and place them in order.
- Stay in the moment.
- Allow your issue or question to be in the forefront of your mind.
- Turn over the cards.
- Take a moment to look at each one. Notice if one jumps out at you more than another. Consider what place it holds in the layout. Pay attention to the symbols on each card and also notice if any jump out at you. Read the descriptions of each card offered in the accompanying book. Allow yourself to be open to what wants to be heard.

- Don't forget to take notes about your reading! I like to take a photo of the layout too.

Notes: _____

_____

_____

_____

_____

_____

_____

_____

_____

Consulting the *I Ching*

Another way you can let guidance in is to consult the *I Ching*. While the image-based tarot helps guide us through compelling issues in our life by tapping into our subconscious symbolically, the *I Ching* can provide more clarity for a particular problem, using words to deliver the message.

These days the *I Ching* is my favored divination tool. I love that I can ask a specific question. Also, while I think of myself as visually oriented, I appreciate how impactful words can be in reaching my subconscious.

There are plenty of books to help you learn this ancient tool. Here, because this was an essential part of my path, I offer a brief description and the basics to get started. Although I describe the steps, you will still need a translation book containing the key to the hexagrams and their interpretations to complete a reading. (See Appendix C for a recommendation.)

The *I Ching* uses numbers to create a unique pattern corresponding to a particular written message called a hexagram—each marked by a number and representative name. There are sixty-four hexagrams. A hexagram is six lines long, consisting of two segments of three lines each: an upper and lower "trigram," (each with its own name). There are four types of lines: broken, solid, changing broken, and changing solid. A changing line turns into its opposite, generating a second hexagram. So, if a reading includes changing lines, a second hexagram will provide more information about the direction an issue could be heading.

Example of a hexagram

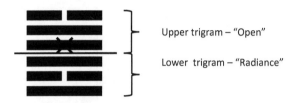

Upper trigram – "Open"

Lower trigram – "Radiance"

49: Skinning/Revolution – about stripping away the old and letting new life emerge

Picture 1. Hexagram 49 with changing line

The hexagram above has a changing line, shown by the X, so it is in the process of changing into another hexagram, #63, where the fourth line from the bottom is a broken line.

63: Already Fording

Picture 2. Hexagram 63

Having a particular question in mind with the *I Ching* is very helpful. Below, I describe how you might go about consulting the *I Ching*. While writing this chapter, in addition to doing the tarot card reading above, I also did an *I Ching* reading about writing this book. (See Appendix C.)

If you do this yourself, allow the words of the interpretive text from your book to sit with you — see what words jump out at you and resonate. Many words might be used, but particular ones may jump out at you. Pay attention to those.

Choose a method.

There are different methods for consulting the *I Ching*. The traditional approach is to use fifty yarrow sticks. Collecting yarrow sticks can be a beautiful rite of passage. I've done this and recommend it, but it is labor intensive, both in collecting and using them as a divination tool. A complicated sequence of events to arrive at the hexagram involves dropping and separating the sticks into various bundles and counting the remaining ones to determine each line.

A second standard method is to use three coins. This method is fast and easy but does not offer the same mathematical randomness as the yarrow sticks.

A third and my preferred method is less known, but it has the advantage of being as mathematically random as the sticks, almost as fast as the coins, and delightfully tactile. That is the method I will describe here. Some people call it the sixteen-token method; I call it the stones method.

The Stones Method of *I Ching* divination

You will need sixteen stones, all about the same size but distinguished by four different colors: seven of one color, five of another, three of another, and one of the fourth color. You could also find stones about the same size and paint a dot on each one. I use small semi-precious stones shaped into little oval cabochons:

7 (white) moonstone – broken line
5 (green) labradorite – solid line

3 (blue) lapis lazuli – changing solid line
1 (orange) sunstone – changing broken line

Creating a hexagram

Each stone represents one of the six lines in the hexagram. As you draw the stones one at a time, you keep track of what kind of line the stone represents. As you create the hexagram, you start at the bottom. So, the first stone drawn represents the bottom line, the next one is the second from the bottom, the third is the third from the bottom, and so on.

The first three selected form the lower trigram, while the next three form the upper trigram. Typically, the *I Ching* books have a graph of the hexagrams. One axis is for the lower trigrams, and one is for the upper. Together they make up a hexagram designated by a particular number and name that you can look up in your book.

The practice:

- Select the stones.
- Hold the stones in your hand or in a little pouch. Without looking, select one, make a note, and replace it. Repeat five more times, keeping track of the order.
- Create the hexagram.
- Each stone represents one of the six lines in the hexagram. You start at the bottom.
- Read the interpretation for the first hexagram and all of the related text for that hexagram.
- There are many different translations. I prefer the one translated by Stephen Karcher (referenced in Appendix C). Go with whatever resonates with you.
- Look up the significance of the changing line.
- Consider the second hexagram and read the initial description only.

- Don't forget to take notes. I like to dedicate a separate journal to my readings.

Notes: _____

_____

_____

_____

_____

_____

_____

_____

_____

Practice #13: Stretching Our Limits — "Is That So?"

As we discussed at the start of this chapter, we have been practicing embarking on an inner striptease that reveals to us the difference between being naked and naked being — investigating the difference between feeling naked and ashamed, and feeling naked and alive. So first, we've talked about how we go about feeling awash in love by re-accessing an experience of naked reverence. Then we looked at what it feels like to let guidance in — to be humbled and open to forces other than our small selves — to learn to pay attention to the synchronicities as they arise, and even to consider opening ourselves to the mystical arts of esoteric divination.

Now I want to get back into our bodies. I want to talk about the juicy potential of stretching our physical limits beyond anything we may have considered before. I want to talk about interrupting all our ideas about who we are and what we are capable of. This shift will require stepping outside our physical comfort zone and pushing the edges of discomfort — like when you are first with another person, in the bedroom, and the clothes are coming off. We are going to expose ourselves to brand-new experiences intentionally. We will dare to be vulnerable and exposed.

When we embark on this level of an inner striptease, we intentionally practice shedding limiting beliefs that have been defining us up to this point. Instead, we challenge what we think we know about ourselves.

For years, I confidently declared, "I don't jog." I supported my "truth" by believing a host of unconscious side thoughts: "I hate jogging." "I never get better at it." "The runner's high will never happen to me." "My knee is damaged." "I have a heart murmur."

During high school, my least favorite part of PE was running around the track. I always finished last or close to last. When I ran, I gasped. I struggled for the entire required two laps. If you saw me, you would notice I looked odd jogging. My body language showed my displeasure and my non-investment. Most runners close their fists as they run, focusing the energy of pumping their arms. I didn't do that. Instead of even lightly closing my fists, I let my wrists dangle loosely, each step costing me additional energy as my wrists flopped. There was no energy, no power in my running. It felt torturous. I hated it and convinced myself I sucked at it.

Secretly, though, I loved imagining myself running. I imagined catching the runner's high I had read about. I envisioned myself as svelte and fit, like all the runners I knew. In books, my favorite characters rose at 5 a.m. and went for a jog before starting their day.

But not me.

Much as I coveted the idea of being a runner, not jogging had become part of who I thought I was.

But when I suddenly realized I didn't know *anything* during my mid-life crisis, I began reinventing myself. My therapist first gave me the idea to start trying new things out. "Just try doing something different," she said. I didn't know what that would look like, but it was great advice.

One weekend, we took the kids camping. My husband and I were a couple of months post-affair and very tentative with one another, but we were still together, and, on this occasion, we were trying out a little family vacation.

The air was stifling between us. I could barely breathe. I felt like I was stepping on eggshells, afraid to say or hear the wrong thing. So many thoughts were clamoring in my head. Does he still love me? Are we going to make it? What about our beautiful family? Who am I without him?

In the face of these challenging questions, I felt paralyzed and helpless.

Who am I? Who are we? I had no idea.

As these thoughts were clamoring in my head that Saturday morning while we were camping as a family, I recalled what my therapist had said about trying something new. I was so uncomfortable in the skin I was wearing that day that I figured nothing could make it worse. So, I turned to my husband and asked if he would watch the kids for a bit.

"I'm going for a run," I declared.

He looked at me like I had grown a second head. A run?

I took off on that run, and as I did, I felt myself draw my hands into lightly closed fists instead of loose dangling wrists. My body could feel it. Something was happening. Something new. Who was this person taking control of this body?

Wait! the inner voices were screaming. "We don't run. We hate running!"

But I kept running anyway. I could barely breathe, but I kept going. My legs burned. My lungs burned, but I held those hands in fists, not dangling, empowering my run.

Who is this person jogging?

My run resembled a very slow jog. Nothing about the run felt good. I was out of my comfort zone, doing something I had told myself for decades that I wasn't good at—that I hated. But even so, as I ran, I felt emboldened.

Some of me registered that stripping away an old identity had great potential. If I was jogging intentionally, then maybe anything was possible.

This simple transformation of who I thought I was—a "non-jogger"—into a slow-running fool in a backwoods campground in Washington during the middle of my darkest days—turned the "I don't know who I am" terror into something full of potential. My fearful thoughts began to follow my body's lead.

Maybe I am a runner, and I didn't know it.
Maybe I will find my way.
Maybe we will find our way back to each other.

Something magical happens when we stretch our limits past what we think we are capable of. And while I appreciate the mystical arts, good old-fashioned science backs me on this one. Dr. Daeyeol Lee, professor of Neuroscience and Psychological Brain Studies at Johns Hopkins, has studied what happens when we push the edges of discomfort. What he shows is that learning happens, and we become happier. When we experience something new, we activate a unique part of the brain that releases dopamine—the happy chemical.

It's one of life's great ironies; to be happy, we need to push the edges of our discomfort and foray into new experiences.

I remember this lesson, which has become a founding part of my guidelines. I sum up my self-motto this way:

• befriend yourself,
• be kind to others,
• say *yes!* to life, and
• cultivate Write Mind Now.

We are talking about the third principle, "Say *yes!* to life." To first order, it reminds me to accept everything as it comes. It reminds me that life will have hard times—people get sick, relationships struggle, and pandemics come along. But when I approach these challenging times with an attitude of openness and willingness, I am much better prepared to respond than when I waste energy resisting and arguing with what is. But there is a secondary reminder here too. And that has to do with being open to trying new things out.

A little inner voice that day said "Let's go jogging." Immediately, the negative voices in my head told me why that was a bad idea and why jogging wasn't part of who I was. Those voices, it turns out, were wrong. Though they speak with authority and have lots of reasoning, they are not the final say.

So, these days, I practice noticing those naysayer voices in my head clothing me in "No!" and practice saying yes instead. Why not? If I am going to reveal myself to myself, I need to be willing to take off the pre-conditioned layers of no clothing.

What does this look like today? It looks like saying yes when my daughter suggested I try rock climbing. I was in my fifties at the time. Rock climbing put me well outside my comfort zone. I was physically unfit and afraid of heights. For months on the first climb of each session, I confronted a psychological barrier when I reached a certain level above the ground. My body would shake, and tears would roll. I knew I was physically safe since the ropes held me, but mentally I was a mess. Still, stretching my mind and pushing myself outside my self-imposed comfort zone worked. I love climbing now. Climbing makes me feel strong and empowered. Rock climbing takes me to places of stunning beauty I would never have seen otherwise and reinforces the understanding that when I leave my comfort zone, I grow.

I use rock climbing in many of my examples because people who haven't tried it tend to have very particular ideas about why they aren't going to try it. I have never been more surprised than when I learned I *love* rock climbing. And I have watched countless others overcome their belief that they would never do rock climbing.

The counterintuitive thing about rock climbing is this: it is unlikely you will get hurt when you first learn. On the ropes, you can only ever fall a few inches. It is one of the safest things I have done with my aging body, and it has successfully gotten me much more robust. I like to encourage people to try rock climbing because it feels like an extreme sport—and once we accomplish something that was once a hard no, many new doors open.

I've seen many amazing scenes at rock-climbing gyms. I've seen a woman with one arm climbing and a guy with a prosthetic leg climbing. However, one of the most heartwarming scenes I have ever seen was an older man in our local gym, Mesa Rim. What I believe was a brother and sister duo in their twenties or thirties was working with him. He looked to be in his seventies. They had gotten him into a harness, climbing up the beginner's wall. They were shouting impassioned words of encouragement to him. "You got this, Dad! That's right, just reach for one more hold! We got you."

The older man was about twenty feet up the wall, giving it his all. He would reach, slip, and then try again, inching his way up the wall. His entire body was shaking, particularly his hands, which could barely grab onto a hold through the shaking. But he was doing it. That man had Parkinson's. As a group of us saw what was happening, we all turned to watch the incredible scene unfold, tears streaming down our faces. He was no longer just an older man with Parkinson's; he was a rock climber.

We inherently know the power of going beyond what we think is possible. So, we rally behind people who stretch their limits. These are our heroes:

- an amputee skiing with prosthetics;
- an eighty-two-year-old woman with bad feet who walks five hundred miles to combat the grief of losing her husband of sixty years to Alzheimer's;
- the guy who falls into a hole, has his arm trapped by a giant rock, and saws his arm off to survive;
- the one who climbed El Capitan a three-thousand foot wall in Yosemite — without ropes; and
- the refugee who walked a thousand miles seeking a better life for her children.

We wear our "no's" like armor protecting us, but more likely, they keep us from growing, shielding us from living a juicy, vital life.

If we want to learn to live naked in the now, we need to be willing to dig past our instinctual no. We need to stretch our limits. We need to practice saying yes.

This encouragement is not a suggestion to be foolhardy—to say yes when someone is abusing you, or to jump off the edge of a cliff willy-nilly. Instead, it's something more refined than that. It is an attitude that we can practice in the physical world by trying new things out, such as I did with jogging and rock climbing, but it extends much further than that.

It is about questioning the limitations we have set for ourselves—both physical and mental. It is about learning to question everything. Doing this softens us. It forces us to begin asking what we think we know to be true. It reminds us that we don't see what we can do until we try. Before we shut down life with a resounding no, we can soften and investigate. We can question our "truths." We can examine our identity. We can be free to reinvent ourselves at any moment. This attitude is living naked in the now—living on the brink of potential.

Buddhists have a helpful saying for remembering this.

Whenever you are faced with a declarative thought or judgment, to reopen the door of possibility, ask yourself, "Is that so?"

I can't jog. *Is that so?*

I'm afraid of heights, I can't climb. *Is that so?*

He shouldn't have forgotten to take out the trash. *Is that so?*

She should have called me back. *Is that so?*

With this practice, I interrupt my conditioning. First, I pause for a moment. Then, I open the door to investigate; what do I know to be absolutely true?

Our goal on this journey of self-inquiry is to practice stretching our limits—to interrupt our conditioned responses to life.

There are lots of simple things we can do. For instance, we could take a different route to the grocery store or practice writing with our non-dominant hand. We could taste something new or dive into a new hobby.

When we are naked in the now, we practice being flexible. We put on and take off identities, thoughts, and beliefs, like clothes. We remain open. We practice saying yes to life, no matter how it looks.

In the last six years, I have embraced the new identity of "rock climber." My daughter has married one of the world's most famous rock climbers. It is one of our favorite family activities. At the end of 2020, we sold our home in Alpine to move to the desert to be closer to world-class rock climbing in Red Rock Canyon.

But recently, I have also been challenged to let go of my grip on that identity.

In early 2021, my husband broke his foot the day before the sale of our house closed. Suddenly, it became apparent that we wouldn't be doing much rock climbing, at least for a while. He is my belay partner, and while I might get out time and again, turning our lives over to rock climbing as we had planned was not going to happen. But being a rock climber is part of who I am now, my brain cried. I have to rock climb to be happy!

Is that so?

During this period, I had to reach beyond my rock-climbing identity. Who am I without climbing every other day?

With extra time on my hands, I turned my attention back to writing and cooking. Yesterday I dived wholeheartedly into learning how to cook Persian style. My house now smells like saffron and barberry rice. A sabzi ghormeh stew is simmering.

I am about to make labneh from scratch and life feels alive and full of potential. I am a Persian cook! Who knew?

Recently, my antenna engineer husband, Jay, tried writing poetry. Jay hates writing and used to think he hated poetry too. But for a few years, a group of Quaker friends has been reading all kinds of poetry (e.g., Rilke, Rumi, Hafiz, Mary Oliver, Jane Hirshfield, Jeff Foster, Dorothy Walter) and talking about it. We love it when a poet challenges our way of thinking and forces us to examine how their words fit into our life—when we struggle a little to feel what the words mean to us. On a whim, somebody suggested that the group members could try writing poetry for us to discuss. Among us are several writers and a poet, but my husband—the non-writer and engineer who never felt an affinity for poetry—is the only one who decided to give it a go. He said something shifted in him as he thought about getting quiet inside and trying to describe some of his peak moments—his insights—in the form of a poem. It was something he had never considered before. He astounded us with his submissions! This man I have been married to for thirty-seven years managed to surprise me as he revealed his poetic soul.

I invite you to try on some new identity clothes. Do something you have never tried before. Push your physical limits. The body is a beacon of empowerment. Doing something physically or creatively that we thought was impossible is a shortcut to experiencing first-hand what it feels like to challenge what we believe to be true about ourselves.

By the way, I got up at 5 a.m. the other day, and as the fiery orange ball of sun came up behind the desert hills near where I live, and the sky turned a wondrous luminous light pink color, I went jogging.

On our inner striptease journey and as a way of learning how to stretch our limits and challenge our conditioning, I encourage folks to begin examining everything they think they know to be true. Then, on your own, ask yourself, *Is that so?*

Whenever you feel particularly righteous, ask yourself, *Is that so?* You might follow it up with, *Can I know with absolute certainty that that is so?*

This kind of self-inquiry can be transformational, though hard to do. We don't like questioning our hard-earned beliefs. (Byron Katie has a wonderful practice of questioning your thoughts called "The Work" as described in her book, *Loving What Is*.) We don't have to relinquish any idea—only look and see if it is still valid for us and whether it is causing us suffering. Challenging our beliefs, especially our beliefs about ourselves, can be wildly empowering and shift us from one way of being to another.

Let's stretch ourselves wide open. Let's look at our limiting beliefs about our ability or interest in doing or not doing something—particularly physical or creative endeavors. (Remember the man with Parkinson's who took up rock climbing anyway?) Now is an excellent time to venture out of our comfort zone.

The practice:

- Consider what areas you have closed off from yourself, such as sports or artistic endeavors.
- Then, think about some that you have never even tried.
- Take a look at your thoughts about these things. They might look like this:
  - I can't dance.
  - I'm afraid of heights.
  - I'm not strong.
  - My arms are weak.
  - I am not artistically inclined.

- ◦ I can't walk long distances.
- ◦ I hate running.
- ◦ I'm not flexible.
- ◦ I'm uncoordinated.
- ◦ I have no affinity for poetry.
- ◦ I'm too (fill in the blank) fat, old, weak, undisciplined to...
- • Pick one limiting belief and decide to challenge yourself.
- • Start by saying the (limiting belief) sentence to yourself, allowing a pause, and then asking yourself, *Is that so? Can I know that is so?*
- • Then, dive further in instead of shrinking away from any activity that makes you feel self-doubt.
- • Fully explore the belief by *intentionally* engaging in something that previously made you feel a certain way.

Some ideas

If you are afraid of heights or feel weak, you might seek out a beginner class in rock climbing.

If you feel uncoordinated or inflexible, you might try dancing, yoga, or martial arts.

If you love math, but hate writing, enroll in a writing practice class. Or, if you love writing but hate math or computers, take a beginning programming class or tutorial on using computers.

If you hate getting outside because you are not "outdoorsy" or physically fit, you might join a meet-up hiking group, an REI class, or a training group at a gym. (With Covid situations improving, indoor arenas should be opening up again. But many sports have outdoor options.)

If you are risk averse, maybe consider skydiving, bungee jumping, or something else that scares you.

Your brain will likely say, "I've tried it a bunch of times before. I'm just no good at it!" Ask, *Is that so?*

Instead consider this:

- Maybe you didn't have proper instruction.
- Perhaps you've had an inner shift since the last time you tried.
- Maybe you discover you enjoy it even though you will never be a superstar at it.
- The goal is to open yourself up by surprising yourself. Just try it—no big deal. Remember, it's like putting on new clothes for a day.
- Pat yourself on the back for going up against well-worn conditioning when you do!

Brainstorming Notes: _____

_____

_____

_____

_____

_____

_____

_____

_____

_____

Practice #14: Exploring Our Depths—Bone Breathing

Thus far on our inner striptease, we've dipped into the idea of naked reverence—being humbled and awash in love before forces more fantastic than our ego self. Then, we visited the concept of letting guidance in, practicing dropping the girding of knowledge we carry that holds the mystery of life at bay and opening ourselves to the possibility of answers revealing themselves organically outside the thinking mind. In the last section, we returned to our bodies and investigated what would happen if we stretched our pre-conditioned limitations and asked, "Is that so?" whenever a hard no came up in our thinking.

We will examine further what we think we know to be true about ourselves. We will dive deeper and expand further than we might have thought possible. We will investigate through our direct experience the power of attention and the experience of naked awareness.

Hold on to your hats, for we want to boldly "proceed without knowing or expectation" about what we might encounter. It is a journey sure to blow your mind.

Before we do, however, I want to point back at the term I just used. These words "proceed without knowing or expectation" came to me in a flash of stunning clarity one day while on a silent retreat in the Sierra Nevada. I suddenly saw that a whole world opens in the gap between thoughts and perception, but that opening to something more is typically filtered by layers of knowing and expectation. I think I see how the next moment will look. I think I know more or less what to expect. I think I know who and what I am. But in a singular moment, this knowing was blown open, revealing a much vaster, seamless world in which there was only potentiality.

It is no wonder that I filter my world with layers of knowledge, and expectation, for this is the training I have received growing up in society.

In our society, we bow before statistics, finding comfort in the fact that weather experts can analyze the conditions and predict with great success what the likelihood of rain is, for instance. We appreciate that doctors have accumulated knowledge about the likely progressions of disease such that when we are sick, we long to hear the odds for our getting better. We invest our money based on forecasts of the economy. As humans living in a shared society, we collect data and study, seeking to improve our lives. We create fine-tuned models and algorithms and use these to predict the future and analyze the past better.

This work is essential. It allows us a certain freedom to play in the world. We can plan trips and organize work schedules more efficiently; we can consider the likelihood that any particular path may be detrimental and correct the course accordingly. Predictions and statistics can allow us to prepare mentally and physically for what may come.

As important as this is for human society, however, it is not an avenue that opens us up to the mystery of life. It is not an avenue that deepens our self-inquiry practice. For that, we have to let go of our expectations. To sally forth on our grand journey to naked awareness, we must let go of what we think we know. By that, I mean what we believe to be "true" because it is statistically likely—and instead deeply investigate our own direct experience.

In a way, we must become pure, unsullied scientists studying the nature of our own consciousness, our own body/mind connection, without the benefit of the "knowledge" of others, relying only on our own experience.

In the last section, I encouraged us to get back into the body and to stretch the limits of what we believed might be possible to allow yet unknown juicy potential to emerge. Typically, when we do something physically that we don't think we can do, we fully engage our senses and get present. So, if I take up rock climbing, I will become finely tuned to the feel of rock under my fingers, aware of the sun's heat or the cool shade. I will listen intently to instructions or encouragement someone might give me. Then, as I reach for an intimidating next handhold, most likely, I will be very present for this particular moment because if I'm not, I will probably fall.

Now, we are going to go deeper.

We will push our inquiry out further than we have done thus far, then direct our attention further inward than we have done so far. We will investigate the power of our attention and the nature of our naked awareness.

To do so, we must let go of everything we think we know.

We are going to start by playing with the power of attention. Attention is something we take for granted. But much like the breath, it is happening naturally, involuntarily, getting captured by something that arises. So, for example, a sudden loud metal crashing noise will cause us to startle and turn our attention toward it. Immediately thoughts will appear. What was that? Was there a car crash in front of the house? I wonder if anyone is hurt? Maybe I should check? Never mind, it was just the wind toppling over the garbage can.

But we can also intentionally direct our attention. For example, right now, I suggest you put your attention on your right foot; immediately, you will be able to do so. Or I can tell you to listen for the next sound to arise, and you will bring all your attention to the act of listening.

Attention is a powerful tool in our self-inquiry practice.

We have probably all heard of the body/mind connection. In this context, we will investigate what role attention plays in the body/mind connection.

Remember how having an adult kiss your "boo-boo" made it feel better? I posit this because of the healing power of attention. When we focus on something, we consciously and intentionally tap into the unseen life-force energy—what the mystics call "primal energy"—that animates all of existence. Some call this the pulse of awareness itself. It's known by different terms in different cultures, such as "prana" to Hindus, "chi" to Chinese, "holy spirit" to Christians, "ruah" in Hebrew, "mana" in Polynesian, and "anima" in Latin. Some say it is the vibration between atoms. Not sure if you buy it? Don't worry; we will experience it for ourselves in the simplest ways. I offer these terms not to introduce something further for you to believe in but to aid in talking about the unseen.

In the next practice session, we will investigate the power of attention alone to enliven our prana field. As we go, please consider for yourself how to describe this experience. Without needing to understand what is happening, how might you describe it? Would you describe it as the underlying energy or pulse of awareness itself?

There are many different practices you might engage in to enliven this field. A popular one is Pranayama, an intentional breath-control exercise common to some yogic practices. There are many different techniques. Some examples include the following:

- alternate nostril breathing (where you block off one nostril and breathe in through the other, then block off the other nostril and breathe out and repeat);
- circular breathing (where you connect the inhale and exhale continuously without allowing for gaps); and
- 4-7-8 breathing (where you inhale through the nose for a count of 4, hold for 7, then exhale forcefully through a pursed mouth for 8).

But I want to share with you something else. It is a new technique for me, though it is an ancient legacy of Taoist masters. It has the remarkable possibility of showing us the power of Pranayama practice and the power of attention. I also like that my mind balked when I first heard of it because it didn't "make sense." It's called bone breathing.

I've been thinking about bones lately because my husband, Jay, just broke his foot, the fifth metatarsal. It can be one of the slowest-to-heal bones because the area is under-circulated.

As I mentioned in the last section, Jay's broken foot has caused us an unexpected hiatus from rock climbing—something we love to do. During this rock-climbing hiatus, I have been diving into cooking new dishes from around the world (Persian last week, Cambodian this week) and also diving headlong into strengthening Jay's body/mind connection, particularly with respect to bones. From one perspective, it feels like our bones are so far away and out of control of our ability to aid in healing. We can alternate heat and cold and elevate our limbs, etc. Still, to first order, if we break a bone, we go to a doctor, have them set the break, and then wait, right? But with this latest break, since it was such a critical limb for rock climbing, Jay and I became interested in what the ancient mystics had to say that might aid in healing. Jay had the instinct himself. He said he felt he needed to use this time off to engage in more Pranayama (breathwork)—something we knew to revitalize the life-force energy. So, we began researching and discovered that there is a very specific Pranayama, especially for healing bones, called bone breathing.

Breathing deep into my belly or regulating my breath in one way or another made some sense to me. But breathing into the bones? What does that even mean? Nonetheless, we were motivated to participate in healing his body, and this was an ancient mystical practice designed especially for that. Why not try it?

For the next six weeks, we practiced bone breathing; it became a fundamental part of our morning meditation practice—a piece I looked forward to. I was astonished each day by the sheer power of attention combined with the breath. It's not that I can swear that the bone breathing helped Jay's bone heal (although the orthopedic surgeon said it was healing well), but rather that it was an enlivening practice all on its own.

Bone breathing reminds me of the power of kissing a boo-boo better. We acknowledge the hurt, accept it, and love it with our attention. Meanwhile, we observe what else happens when we do. The Taoist masters say bone breathing (also known as bone marrow breathing) is beneficial for repairing bones and opening the human potential to its maximum. Here's to more of that!

On the journey today, not only will we witness the power of attention to travel into the deep marrow of our bones, but we will also investigate the nature of our body in the context of awareness only.

We all have a rough idea of who we are. We seem to be a collection of thoughts, ideas, emotions, and memories housed in a physical vessel called a "body," right? We might call this our personal body/mind. At first, it feels like each of us is a distinct and discrete entity.

In this practice, we will look closely at the expectation that we know who and what we are. We will extend the "Is that so?" question to this most fundamental of beliefs. We will investigate if we can discern where we begin and end. We are going to look for our boundaries.

When I first did this, I reasoned, if I am a "something"—a discrete body/mind—there should be edges or boundaries to our existence, right?

Well, that's easy, you say. My boundary is my skin.

Is that so?

Let's investigate by looking closely at our direct experience—not the one we have been told about, but the one of which we alone are aware—and see what we find.

We'll start by diving into the deep, unseen interior of our bodies—the very marrow of our bones—with this introduction to bone breathing, allowing our bones to come alive. And then, we will expand outward to investigate the edges of our experience in a simple experiment that enlivens our field of awareness, inviting the question, "Where do I start and end?"

We will consider the power of attention and the nature of awareness when we let go of our ideas of what is possible and who we are, naked in the now.

The practice:

- To start, find a comfortable seated position and remove your shoes and any tight clothing.
- Now, bring your attention right here. Take a moment to relax. Drop your shoulders, close your eyes, and rest your hands gently on your lap. Intentionally breathe in through your nose into your belly. Try giving a little jiggle to the torso encouraging it to release any tension. Notice the ground beneath your feet and the chair beneath your seat.
- To further center us and to warm up the power of our attention, let's ring a gong (you can find one on the Insight and other apps). Follow the sound of that gong until it completely fades.
- Listen carefully as it fades. Notice the bright expansion that happens when the sound fades completely.
- Now allow your hands to rest face up in your lap, the fingers stretched open, the palms open.
- Begin breathing slowly through the nose. Inhale, then exhale. Simple breathing.

- Bring your attention now to the tip of the left index finger. Relax the wrist, hand, and fingers.
- With your next breath, I want you to imagine breathing into the tip of that finger, allowing the attention to travel from the end to its base as you inhale. Then exhale normally through the nose, letting the energy stay in the finger but returning your attention to the tip of the finger. Breathe in, allowing your attention to move slowly from the tip, imagining the breath moving up the inside of the finger and then, with the exhale returning attention down and back to the end tip.
- Just continue breathing into your index finger for a few more breaths.
- Now, please notice what that finger feels like. Is there a heaviness or warmth in that finger?
- Compare it to what the right index finger feels like. Does it feel different? Do you notice a warm, heavy tingling throughout the left index finger that is noticeably different from the right? Notice how the left index finger feels compared to the right.
- Now continue the practice. Breathe into each of the fingers of the left hand, either one at a time or all at once. Breathe into the fingers to their base, then exhale back to the tips.
- As the left hand becomes warmer and heavier, compare it with the right hand, where we have not breathed yet.
- Now move your attention to the right hand and repeat the practice on that side, starting first with the right index finger. Once both hands feel heavy, continue the same method but move the attention higher and higher in the arms until the same feeling is up to the shoulders.
- Now move the practice to your toes, feet, and legs. Guide awareness up the toes singly or together to the ankle.

(Because Jay and I were working on healing the small fifth metatarsal bone of his right foot, we very specifically focused on that, bringing our attention to the pinkie toe on the right side and directing attention up the bone to the base of the foot.)

- Notice the difference between bringing attention to the index fingers and the pinkie toes. (For me, it took a bit longer to experience a sensation in the foot than in the finger.) Just keep breathing into the right pinkie toe and up the foot. Allow attention to move from the toe up the outside edge of the foot to the ankle.

- Continue the practice until the area feels enlivened — warm, heavy, tingling.

- On your own, continue to guide your awareness up the toes of the left foot until you have enlivened both feet; then continue to practice moving the attention up both legs.

- You can continue this practice by breathing up your spine as well. Begin at the base of the sacrum and run your awareness up the spine until you reach the bottom of the neck, allowing the same feeling of warmth, tingling, and heaviness to develop.

- This powerful and sweet meditative practice helps us feel the body/mind connection for ourselves. When we move our attention to an area of the body, that area becomes enlivened, and we can feel a vitality that we usually take for granted and of which we are unaware. After practicing, jot down what you noticed.

Notes: _____

_____

_____

_____

_____

_____

_____

_____

_____

Practice #15: Naked Awareness—How Far and How Deep Do I Go?

Let's continue our practice today with another simple experiment that introduces the question "Where do I begin and end?"

The practice:

- For this experiment, I want you to gently clasp your hands and let them rest nestled together in your lap.
- Now, let's take a moment to bring our attention back to the body, as it may have wandered into the mind thinking about the last exercise we did. Close your eyes.
- Drop your shoulders, relax your cheekbones and forehead, squirm slightly in your seat, wriggle your neck a little, and notice the ground beneath your feet.
- Draw a nice, easy breath in through your nose into your belly. Repeat a few times. Notice the gentle rise of your chest and shoulders as you breathe in and the falling as you breathe out.
- Now, I want you to draw your attention to the intersection of your seat on the chair. Just notice. In your mind's eye, you can probably visualize your bottom resting on the chair, but instead of focusing on that visual, I want you to tune into the sensations. What do you physically feel? Can you distinguish where your body ends and the chair begins? Is there something you can point to that marks the distinction between the two? Is there an impression that you are taking up more space than what you know your body to be taking up?
- Keep noticing, asking yourself, where do I begin and end?
- Now, draw your attention to your clasped fingers resting gently on your lap. Intellectually you know

you have interlaced your fingers, but what is your experience of them now? Can you tell where one finger ends and another starts? Now focus on the body as a whole and ask yourself, where do I begin and end? Am I confined to any boundaries? Is there a hard limit where I no longer am?

- For a moment, check in with your sense of self. Is your sense of self confined to the strict boundaries of your body, or does it seem to cross over and diffuse into space—more like dye spreading outward in a body of water?

- As you feel the boundaries of the body blurring in relation to the physical world around it, ask yourself whether you, too, seem to extend beyond the physical limitations of the body. Let yourself let go of the idea that the body is a container into which you are poured. If that is not entirely true, what is true?

- If your sense of self extends beyond the body—beyond the brain, which we intellectually understand to control the body—what might that mean to you?

- Ask yourself, what am I? And just like we listened to the gong fade into nothingness, allow even that question to fade into nothingness too.

- Now, bring your attention back to your chest. Unclasp and wriggle your fingers and slowly open your eyes.

- Allow yourself to process this discovery internally as you go about your day. What am I? Where do I begin and end? How do I experience awareness not connected to body or mind?

Notes: _____

_____

_____

_____

_____

_____

_____

_____

Chapter 7

Restore and Rejuvenate Relationships

Healing yourself is connected with healing others.
—Yoko Ono

Our journey to being naked in the now is an inward voyage we can (and ultimately must) take alone, but many of us spend significant time with others along the way. The quality of our relationships can profoundly affect our life, either alleviating or increasing our suffering.

For that reason, I want to spend some time talking about practices that can lessen the separation between you and another, heal hurts, encourage vulnerability, and deepen intimacy. As we tear down boundaries between us and another, we also dive deeper into ourselves. As we offer compassion to another, we also provide it back to ourselves. And when we do so, it is much easier to be present.

We will look at ancient healing meditations and simple practices that can help us heal a broken or struggling relationship or bridge a geographical gap. These practices are for any relationship that needs healing—it could be a relationship with your mother, sister, spouse, lover, or friend. It could even be your relationship with yourself.

In life, we sometimes become estranged from people who were once dear to us. There are several reasons that this can happen. It could be that a loved one is struggling with a mental illness or is under the influence of drug or alcohol addiction. It might be that geographic distance has impacted us. Sometimes, we act as best we can under whatever the circumstances are (stress, illness, conditioning, a global pandemic combined with endemic racism and political polarization), only to discover that a particular behavior or reaction has contributed to a seemingly irreparable rift in a relationship with another. Such splits can be devastatingly impactful.

It can also happen that another has deeply wronged us— perhaps your life has intersected with someone you would never outwardly choose, yet the intersection occurred, and the result has caused deep suffering. We don't think of these as "relationships" per se, yet there is no doubt that we are in a relationship with each other. There is any number of tragic circumstances that might fit this bill—rape, for instance, or bullying. In such cases, we seek wholeness. We want to heal, but we don't know how to start. It may seem nearly impossible to forgive the other, but neither does it feel good to be stuck in a victim identity, giving over our well-being to another.

We will look at a few practices to help us heal ourselves, our relationships, and all that we see as wrong in the world.

Let's practice!

Practice #16: Pink Light Technique

This first technique is specifically designed to restore a rift in a relationship that we hope to repair. It can also help us start to heal from wrongdoing done to us. It is also a sweet moment to connect with ourselves and the people who are important to us.

I first learned this healing meditation from the Ishayas. (I talk about the Ishayas at length in my memoir, *More... Journey to Mystical Union through the Sacred and the Profane*.) I was told it was an ancient healing technique. As for the significance of using *pink* light, some folks claim that pink light is experienced as unconditional love. I once was on a tour of a prison and the guard told me they painted the cells a light pink because it had a calming effect. Anyway, I share it with you as it was shared with me to experiment for your own self. You can do this simple technique anywhere. It takes about five to ten minutes. It does not require you to speak or face another. Once you get the knack of it, you might find it becomes addictive. It can be done daily (I highly recommend that), perhaps just as you are going to sleep at night.

Pink light is one of those healing meditations you do for its own self—an inside job. It gently scours the unhealed corners of the heart of all your relationships and brings them into the light, where healing is possible. I think you will discover that it has the capacity to start inside you and somewhat magically works its way out to the world at large.

I have heard stories of the miraculous power of this technique from those who have experienced abuse. I've heard that runaway children reconnected with their families within weeks of using this technique. I have even heard that people have used this technique on groups of people. One young man was being severely bullied at school. He began using the method on the group of bullies. Eventually, he did his entire school to include everyone contributing to his school-fed suffering. He did this every night and eventually became a well-liked young man—a spokesperson for his peers.

When I first learned the pink light technique, I wanted to heal my relationship with my husband. I hoped to focus on something other than our difficulties after his affair. This technique allowed me to do so.

Since then, I have used it hundreds of times to bring me back to being willing to heal a relationship with another. I've used it after an ordinary fight with my husband, a devastating misunderstanding with my mother, when a dear relative was struggling with their mental health, and on work colleagues. What I have discovered is that it softens my attitude. It changes something inside me helping me to be more compassionate, more loving, and more open—all without interacting directly with the other person at all. It also gives me something to do, which can be an important component for overcoming feeling helpless.

I also used this technique to help me heal from childhood sexual abuse. For weeks, I included the perpetrator in my daily practice of this technique. I believe it contributed to a pivotal healing moment in my journey. I've written about that moment in an essay called "Goodness Through and Through," published in the *Shaking the Tree* anthology, volume 2. The article describes an almost mystical experience that happened spontaneously during a flashback of childhood sexual trauma. Typically, I would spiral into a dark hole after a triggering vision, but this time something extraordinary happened. My perspective changed, and I existed on the edge of my known reality.

Briefly, here's what happened.

As the flashback took over, I was a little girl cowering in one instant. Then, inexplicably, I flew into the man's perspective the next instant. I was now him. I was looking through his eyes down at the child who was me. I saw the scene through his eyes as if I were him. And stranger yet, I felt what he felt. And what he felt was desire. Urgent, hot energy full of longing and passion flowed through my (his) body. Then, just as suddenly, I was the adult me again, a woman on retreat with her husband. My own body stirred—an involuntary response that flooded me with shame.

Then, as if the edges of reality had not bent far enough, I was simultaneously all of us: child, man, and woman. I was the child, afraid and uncertain, trembling in the dark. I was the man whose urgency overtook him, blotting out all reason, ruled by desire. And I was a woman outraged at him, at the circumstance, and betrayed by her body.

I did not identify with any of these points of view for a brief moment. Instead, it was as if I had stepped back calmly, without judgment, witnessing these three different points of view. And, at that moment, a deep well of compassion opened up. I saw us as sharing an untouchable core that was good through and through—notwithstanding criminal behavior. Overcome with compassion, I silently and privately forgave my perpetrator and freed myself.

What I am about to share works because it puts us in an attitude of willingness and openness to extending compassion in both directions, to ourselves and another. We enter a sacred space for a moment when we sit down to do this. We let go of all our ideas of what the other or we did wrong and embrace the simple desire to be back in the innocent space with them and ourselves.

I am not suggesting singing Kumbaya with an abuser, only entertaining a willingness for a gentle softening of the fear and hatred that can freeze our hearts and keep our minds spinning out of the present moment, obsessed with terrible "what if" or "if only" stories.

Pink light gives us a moment to put ourselves in a safe and loving space with others. Please use the technique in innocence and without conditions. It is miraculous!

The practice:

- Let's sit for a moment and come into this moment. Close your eyes. Notice the ground beneath your feet and the chair beneath your seat.
- Now, draw your attention to your breath. Allow yourself to feel the breath traveling in the nostrils, down the throat, and into the belly. Soften your cheekbones, relax your shoulders, and let your eye sockets go.
- Now, in your mind's eye, picture a loving pink light radiating from your heart, encompassing you. Don't worry if you can't visualize a pink light. Some people do, and some people don't. It's the intention that matters. Mentally say, "There is a pink light coming from my heart encompassing me entirely."
- Now bring to mind a loving image of yourself. It could be something that happened this morning or ten years ago. Any small moment will do. It doesn't matter how or why you felt loved, just that you did. If you can't think of any, imagine yourself as a baby newly cradled in loving arms.
- Once you've touched into a loving image of yourself, place that image in front of you outside the pink light sphere, then picture yourself spreading the pink light totally around the image. When the image is covered, let it go.
- Now, we are going to move on to working with others. We will start with someone easy to love at this time—a partner or child, perhaps (or even a pet)—imagine them in front of you, outside the pink light sphere. Imagine

them in a loving memory — a sweet moment. Then, in your mind's eye, picture yourself covering that person with the pink light (as if you were icing a cake). Cover them, and then let them go.

- Now, naturally, allow the image or idea of someone else to come forth. Often, each member of your immediate family or close friends will come to mind. Just see who shows up. Remember them in a loving memory when possible. (If you cannot remember this person in a loving memory, just picture them in front of you. If you cannot do this, bring them in, standing at a distance or facing away from you.)

- Next, bring in anyone with whom you still have an emotional charge or discomfort. (Follow the instructions above.) Again, attempt to remember them in a loving memory. If you can't, you can place them at a distance; if the person is difficult, you can imagine them as an innocent baby.

- Cover them in pink light and let them go.

- Allow anyone else to show up in your mind's eye (whoever comes into your awareness is okay, whether you know them or not), cover them with the pink loving light, and let them go. You might also find that people who have passed come to mind. That's okay. Wrap them up in pink light too, and let them move on.

- Finally, when no one else comes to mind, return to the loving image of yourself. Cover that image of yourself in pink light, then let it go and open your eyes.

Notes: _____

_____

_____

_____

_____

_____

_____

_____

_____

A couple of follow-up comments

Cover anyone who comes to mind in pink light. When you've done that, let the person go, but don't push them away. It's weird, but it becomes like a conveyor belt where people spontaneously and naturally come to mind. You wrap them up in pink light and allow them to move on. Then the next one appears—all effortlessly. You'll see.

Once you have wrapped them up in pink light, you can let them go for the day. You will get a sense when someone is complete and no longer requires treatment. Some people will not show up for a while; others you didn't expect to see will suddenly appear to receive the pink light. And, like the young man I mentioned earlier, you can also do this technique on a group of people. When the young bullied man did this technique, he placed that group of bullies far away in his mind's eye and quickly wrapped them up in pink light. He kept doing it every night for months.

The point is to remain curious.

Who shows up in your mind's eye seeking your pink light?

Try it! And let me know how it goes.

Practice #17: Tonglen—a Compassionate
Practice of Bringing Suffering In

Before I embarked on a spiritual journey, I benefitted from one thing my mother told me. She told me that I had an inviolable golden core. She said that deep inside me was an untouchable place that radiated pure goodness. There was no religious connection with this concept, nor was there any waffling. It's not that she "believed" in a golden core; it's something she had touched and knew to be true.

My mother lived through some tough stuff as a child during World War II in occupied Holland; her family secretly housed Jews at potential peril to themselves, and her mother also worked for the underground war effort as a courier sometimes carrying weapons in her large bag. Just after the war, her parents divorced, when divorce was highly irregular. Afterward, she lived with an abusive stepfather until she ran away from home in her teens. Still, she grew into a wise, kind, and compassionate woman. When she told me I had a golden core, it gave me something to hold on to in my darkest hours, even if I wasn't sure it was real. I can remember in the days following my husband's affair, and later as memories of childhood sexual abuse arose, not being able to feel the ground beneath my feet. I repeatedly took comfort in the idea of my inviolable golden core. I was suffering, no question, yet I retained an untouchable inner core in some unfathomable way. It was a thread of pure potential that offered me much solace.

Many years later, I would learn that this "golden core" has many names around the world, such as "the awakened heart-mind," "vast expanse heart essence," "boundless heart," and "shunyata" (emptiness). It's not something tied to one's thoughts or emotions, nor is it dependent on having certain life circumstances or being "worthy." Instead, it is an undeniable and unshakable radiant and good presence that we habitually overlook. It is the golden core at the heart of naked awareness. And it is a source for ending suffering.

I want to share with you one of the most transformative practices. It is a practice that relies on this golden core of naked awareness to help us cultivate selfless love and compassion. It turns everything we think we know on its head.

In Tibetan Buddhism, it is called Tonglen. Tong means "sending out," and len means "accepting" or taking on. So often, we call it "sending and taking." Many spiritual teachers give Tonglen instruction, notably Pema Chodron (an American Buddhist nun), who calls it the Path of Transformation. Tara Brach (author of *Radical Compassion*) says Tonglen trains us to touch vulnerability and discover the boundless heart space that can be a transformer of sorrows. The Compassion Institute at Stanford University offers Tonglen training and has conducted numerous research studies on the benefits of this kind of compassion training.

So, what is Tonglen? And why is it considered anathema to our usual thinking?

Tonglen is a Tibetan mind-training technique that uses breathing and visualization to help us discover that contrary to our fears, we have access to an unlimited reservoir of healing compassion. It allows us to change our attitude towards pain and open our hearts so we can become more loving as we dissolve the pain surrounding us.

Some describe it as the nuclear weapon of compassion.

Tonglen encourages us to do what we don't want to, go where we don't want to, and embrace what often feels like the unembraceable part of ourselves and others.

Instead of working hard to expel negativity, avoid suffering, and surround ourselves only with the positive, we do the opposite. We intentionally breathe in suffering. When we do it on others, with each in-breath, we willingly take in their pain. With each out-breath, we send out relief to them.

Tonglen helps us end suffering by awakening our compassion and bringing our attention to our inviolable golden core—that untouchable vastness radiating goodness I first heard about from my mom. In Tonglen, we practice breathing suffering and darkness into that vast, pure golden core (not into our thinking mind), and then we breathe out light and relief. Notice, this is very different from a classic New Age tool that says we should breathe in light and positivity and breathe out darkness and negativity.

Tonglen teaches us to look directly at suffering. It teaches us not to fear hardship but to connect with and embrace our suffering and that around us. With Tonglen, we can overcome our fear of misery and dissolve the tightness in our hearts by awakening the well of compassion that is inherent in and shared by all of us.

What I love about it is it changes my mindset. Instead of feeling overwhelmed by events and circumstances, it teaches me to imagine a deep reservoir that can handle anything. It expands upon the solace I felt when my mom told me I had an inviolable golden core. It teaches me to trust and rely on that place, actively seek it out, and access it not only to offer compassion to myself but to loved ones and strangers, even enemies.

There are subtle layers to this transformational tool. It is the one tool I know of that allows us to get into the trenches of suffering with others without becoming entangled in the drama of that suffering. What happens when we do this technique is a softening of our self-centered orientation—hence the description of it as a way to cultivate selfless love and compassion. Tonglen reinforces our willingness to serve others while building inner strength.

There are different approaches to learning this technique. Pema Chodron teaches that one way to begin doing Tonglen is with someone we love dearly. She tells the story of Trungpa Rinpoche (a Tibetan Buddhist master), who saw a puppy being stoned to death by a jeering crowd when he was eight. Afterward, all he had to do was think of that dog, and his heart would instantly open because he would have done anything to breathe in that animal's suffering and to breathe out relief.

But others teach to practice with oneself first, which is how I learned it while on retreat with the Center for Sacred Sciences. The teacher of the retreat explained that in this practice, we would willingly take on the suffering of others while sending out love and compassion to them. "But," he explained, "to do that, we each have to be willing to experience our own suffering fully; otherwise, we cannot develop genuine compassion for others."

I had no idea what to think when I first learned this technique. It sounded pretty simple, so I just followed the instructions exactly. I didn't expect this exercise to propel me to the highest truth of all. Instead, when I felt wholly inadequate, it opened the door and showed me the truth: a luminous, seamless presence in which there was no self and other, only love overlaid with simple delusion. It showed me that Golden Core—not intellectually, but through direct recognition. I previously had thought of it as "my" golden core, but in the highest truth, there is no "I," only love. That Golden Core is the same golden core shared by all without boundaries—genuinely self-less love.

What happened to me was this.

The teacher encouraged us to begin by stabilizing our attention. (In our terminology, this would mean doing one of the juicy practices for getting present, such as following the breath or prayer in the heart.) It's necessary to take the time to get centered and grounded so that you are not overwhelmed by the intensity of feelings that the practice can arouse.

The teacher had us start with ourselves. He said to focus on something that made us feel bad now or to vividly recall something challenging from the past, such as a severe illness or a breakup of a relationship. We could also look for a piece of content in our life that repeatedly caused us suffering. These include things like feelings of unworthiness or inadequacy.

As I settled into the exercise and looked within myself for suffering, I saw that I held on to believing that I was somehow never good enough. Thinking about this initially brought tears to my eyes as I thought how much suffering it caused me to have the ongoing background thought "I am not enough." It caused me to mentally beat myself up repeatedly for not solving problems better, for not loving more perfectly, for making mistakes, for not being dedicated, smart, or pretty enough.

Usually, I might have tried to combat this thought by replacing it with a positive idea—like "I am doing my best" or "I am becoming better and better." But the instructions were unambiguous. We were not turning away from what was causing us suffering; we were embracing it and breathing it directly into our very being.

The teacher cautioned us not to think about the story behind the suffering. We were not to analyze what happened or to get sucked into any mental dramas of justification or blame (another conditioned tendency). He said all of our stories about why we were suffering were things the thinking mind had created to try to make the suffering disappear or to pretend it was not real. In this practice, we were to do the opposite. Instead of rejecting our angst, we were to embrace it and experience it completely.

Because the stories associated with any piece of suffering are so compelling, he taught us to stay focused on the physical sensations of the suffering rather than what we thought about it. He asked us, "Where do you feel it? Stomach? Heart? Throat? Head? What qualities does it have? Heavy? Burning? Hot?

Aching?" He encouraged us to get to know the sensations of this particular piece of suffering as intimately as we would the body of a long-time lover.

I tuned in to the physical sensations connected with the core belief that "I am not enough." I immediately felt a tight ball of fear tied up in my throat. I felt uncomfortable and wanted that feeling to go away. I desperately wanted to think of light, happy thoughts—anything to not experience that overwhelming fear constricting my throat, causing tears to pulse.

But I stayed with the practice.

The teacher guided us, "Next, as you inhale, gather whatever anger, sorrow, or pain you are feeling and breathe it into your heart. If you are good at visualization, you can imagine these feelings as having the form of hot, black smoke. Either way, breathe in deeply and allow the whole dark mass of suffering to dissolve in the space in your heart."

Yikes. Our teacher told us to breathe in imaginary hot, black smoke. I couldn't help but think, shouldn't we be getting rid of that? I was much more used to the idea of expelling dark energy.

I inhaled deeply, and instead of pushing away the hot, black, icky smoke of "I am not enough," I envisioned it coming inside me.

He said, "It does not matter how much suffering you feel or how intense it becomes, because truly speaking, that space in your heart is as infinite as Consciousness itself. So, there is no need to be afraid. On the contrary, the more suffering you can breathe in, the wider your heart will open to accommodate it."

Infinite capacity. I let that sink in, contrasting that potential with feeling tight, constricted, inadequate, and small.

"Now, as you exhale, breathe out love and compassion for yourself. Add a heartfelt wish or prayer that you might be relieved of all your suffering, and instead be filled with boundless joy, peace, and happiness."

Now that sounded better—more like a positive affirmation.

Finally, he instructed us to repeat the process of inhaling suffering and exhaling love and compassion. The idea was not to "think" about what we are doing but to nakedly feel our suffering entering our hearts, dissolving there, and flowing out as selfless love and compassion.

The teacher left us on our own to practice. I began by breathing deeply and practicing prayer in the heart to stabilize my attention. Then I brought my suffering into focus—a tight ball of fear tied up in my throat with the thought "I am not enough." I felt my throat constrict, and with it, I felt panicked and consumed by the fear that I would never be enough and would not get it "right." I wondered if I felt it in my throat because I didn't trust myself to speak the truth. I desperately wanted to push that feeling away instead of letting it in. My training had taught me to argue with the thought "I am not enough," and instead encourage myself with praise. "You are enough! Look at what good you do. Look at how you care for others." I wanted to do anything other than embrace the thought "I am not enough." But I kept on with the practice and imagined bringing those words into my heart space. I didn't even really know what that meant, so I mentally said the words and tried to imagine them moving out of my throat, deeper into my being, into my heart—my golden core. I focused intensely on the physical sensations of the feeling—the pulsing tears behind the constricted throat. The dense, impenetrable tight ball of fear blocked my throat, causing what felt like an actual lump. It felt like a sword pierced my throat. Negative thoughts about the practice kept coming up: This is stupid. This is a bad idea. This isn't helping even a little bit. This is making me feel worse.

But then, as I persisted with the exercise, suddenly, there was a flash of what I can only describe as "emptiness." It was just a moment of awareness of something vast and empty behind my heart. Immediately my mind labeled that emptiness as "nothing" and further declared, "There's nothing there to help you with this problem." But something shifted slightly in my deeper awareness as I recognized that perhaps that "emptiness" was not nothing so much as the infinite space in my heart into which these feelings would dissolve. So, I ignored my thoughts and returned to bringing the "I am not enough" into that space.

Then, just behind the thinking mind's declaration, there was a 180-degree shift, and these words dropped in with utter clarity: "I am inadequate." But the words were dripping with truth—not blame—simple, unadorned truth.

The words I hated and fought so much suddenly were on their heads. Finally, the Truth hit me: "I am not enough." As a self-centered ego identity, all the mechanisms, thoughts, and attempts to control are not enough—nor will they ever be enough. They can't be, but pure unadulterated love and compassion are.

I suddenly saw that my identification with a "problem-solving-ego-I" rather than identifying with that vast, empty heart space was the problem. Ego-I is inherently finite and will always, on some level, be inadequate. It will always look for problems to solve instead of resting in the moment's perfection. But that vast, open, pure space of the heart ever flowing with love and compassion is boundless and inherently peaceful. It is always enough.

As the fundamental truth hit me that who I thought I was (a separate person with important thoughts and ideas) is inadequate and will always be insufficient, the "Who am I?" quest of a spiritual journey came rushing in. And with that realization came pure freedom.

I am not who I think I am. I am that emptiness itself. I am the golden core. I am love and compassion itself.

With this realization came a sense of awe and an incredible lightness of being, a buoyancy—energy without any vibration, and a sense of loving invincibility. There was no sense of self. Thoughts were still happening, but they were on the periphery, and I no longer identified with them. The dramas of life were innocent delusions of the ego, and there was only compassion—sweet, gentle, impersonal. The emptiness was full. It was everything. It was utterly unadorned nakedness, and I was it.

I realize this may sound somewhat fantastical, my friends, so rest assured there are much simpler benefits to doing Tonglen than recognizing Oneness.

As reported by the Compassion Institute, Stanford University research suggests that consistent Tonglen practice can lead to increased happiness, calmness, acceptance of emotions, self-acceptance, job satisfaction, self-caring behavior, compassion for self and others, openness to receiving compassion from others while decreasing worry and anxiety, anger, mind wandering, emotional suppression, and chronic pain severity.

Pretty good, huh?

As I began to appreciate the power of accepting my own suffering and not bypassing it, I realized this gave me the potential to feel genuine compassion (not pity) for others. So, as instructed, I began to practice Tonglen on others, starting with people I loved and cared for and then moving on to strangers and even enemies. I found myself willing to breathe in any dark, black negativity and breathe out light and relief.

Sending and taking is one of those practices that you can begin to integrate into daily life anytime you see or feel suffering and when you encounter a situation where there is nothing else you can do except engage in this practice.

It may seem insignificant to breathe in suffering and breathe out love and compassion along with a heartfelt wish that they are happy, but it creates a powerful ripple of love that perpetuates.

It also helps dissolve our conditioning by retraining us in how to deal with negativity, seeing ourselves not as self-centered "What about me?" beings but selfless transformational forces that convert hostility to compassion.

This selfless transformational force, my friends, is everything.

The practice (on yourself):

- Start by relaxing. You can use any techniques you've learned in this book or begin by drawing your attention to your body. Notice your feet on the ground. Relax your shoulders, face, eyes, and anywhere that feels tense.
- Do a few minutes of deliberate breathing. A simple practice is called 4, 7, 8 breathwork. You inhale to a count of 4, hold for 7, and breathe out to a count of 8. (See also Appendix A.) Spend a few moments intentionally breathing as described, continually relaxing the body, and noticing the sensations.
- Now, bring to mind your own suffering. This might be as simple as a thought: "I am not worthy," or "She doesn't love me." Or it could be more complicated. Try to recall it as vividly as possible, allowing any feelings to arise. With this act we are allowing ourselves to see our suffering self. We will become the object of our own compassion.
- Once you can feel the suffering, stop thinking about it. Don't analyze why it happened or get sucked into any related drama about it. Our mind creates stories about suffering to make it go away. Here, in this practice, you are going to do the opposite. Instead of rejecting it, you will embrace it and experience it completely. Thoughts will likely still be arising.
- Turn your attention to the physical sensations.

- Ask yourself:
  - Where do I feel it? Is it in my stomach? Heart? Throat? Head?
  - What qualities does it have? Is it heavy, hot, burning, or aching?
- The point (as my teacher said) is to get to know the physical sensations as intimately as you would the body of a long-time lover.
- Inhale your own suffering feelings into your heart. Gather whatever anger, fear, shame, sorrow, or pain you feel and breathe it *into* your heart. Imagine these feelings are hot, black smoke. If you can't visualize that, don't worry; tell yourself you are breathing deeply and allowing the pure space of your heart to dissolve the dark mass of suffering. (Remember, it does not matter how much or how intense the suffering is because this space is infinite consciousness.)
- Breathe out love and compassion for yourself. If you are visual, you can imagine this takes the form of radiant, white light, which you exhale through all the cells of your body so that it envelops you like a warm, luminous cloud. Love and compassion are inherent in consciousness itself, so don't worry about needing to generate special effort. As much as you open your heart to suffering, that is how much love and compassion will flow. Finally, add a heartfelt wish or prayer that you might be relieved of all your suffering and be filled with boundless joy, peace, and happiness.
- Keep going with the process. Feel your suffering being breathed into your heart, dissolving there, and flowing out with the out-breath as selfless love and compassion.
- Do sending and taking for all beings. End by taking in the suffering of all beings as you inhale and sending out selfless love and compassion to all beings as you exhale.

152

- Finish with a heart wish or prayer that all beings in the universe may be relieved of whatever anguish, pain, fear, or sorrow they are experiencing and instead be filled with boundless joy, peace, and happiness.

Notes: _____

_____

_____

_____

_____

_____

_____

_____

The practice (on others):

- The practice (on others) is essentially the same as on yourself except that instead of taking yourself as the object of compassion, you will take on someone else.
- Start by relaxing.
- Do some deliberate breathing to stabilize attention.
- Bring a friend to mind who you know is suffering. Vividly imagine what is going on for them.
- Make a resolve to take on their suffering, so that they may be relieved of all their anguish and pain.
- Inhale their suffering into your heart. Imagine those feelings to be black, heavy smoke. Breathe in deeply and imagine your friend's pain is yours, then allow the angst to dissolve into your heart.
- Exhale love and compassion. With your out-breath, wish that all your efforts will make your friend feel good. Imagine yourself giving them whatever you have that would make them happy—even your own health.

Visualize (if you can) this gift is white light encompassing them. Offer your heartfelt wish that they be relieved of suffering and filled with joy.

- Stay with the process of inhaling suffering and exhaling love and compassion.
- Do sending and taking for all beings.

Notes: _____

_____

_____

_____

_____

_____

_____

_____

_____

Practice #18: Touch Another with Words

More than kisses letters mingle souls.
—John Donne

Thus far in this chapter about investigating tools for restoring and rejuvenating relationships, we have been talking about some powerful if esoteric healing tools: pink light, a simple technique that gently scours the unhealed corners of our relationships and brings them into the light where healing is possible, and Tonglen, an advanced Buddhist practice for taking on suffering, trusting it to dissolve in the infinite expanse of our golden core.

Now we will look at something so mundane we can easily overlook its potential. I am talking about the power of the written word as expressed in a good old-fashioned love letter. I don't mean only love letters written to our intimate beloved, but love letters we may write to our mother, child, dying neighbor, or self. In our digital age of short quips and emojis, and in this recent pandemic era of quarantine, I think of love letters as the long embrace we all desperately need.

Imagine walking up to your mailbox for a moment and finding a physical letter from someone important in your life. Then, imagine taking that letter into your (possibly socially isolated) house, sitting down with a cup of tea or coffee, and reading the words that someone sat down to write to you. Words that were not pithy responses on social media, carefully crafted arguments, or awkward caught-on-Zoom moments, but something else altogether—slowed down, tuned-in words speaking directly about what someone appreciates and loves about you.

Then, imagine being the author of those words and writing to someone else in your life. Who might need to feel the hug of your words?

This kind of writing comes from a different source. It comes from slowing down and finding our still center—from feeling our emotional connection to an issue, to a person, to ourselves. It comes from a place of vulnerability and flow. Love letters escape the boundaries of the thinking mind, the academic culture of structure, and the word-limit boundaries of social media to meander fearlessly through heartfelt territory.

Writing a love letter is as much for the writer as it is for the reader. When we allow words from the heart to flow, we escape the inner critic who constantly compares and judges our writing. We let go of perfection and instead write from the heart. A love letter is more than the stream of consciousness writing in our journal. A love letter has an intended recipient with whom we hope to communicate and connect.

The revitalized power of writing a love letter became apparent a couple of years ago and continues to move me. One day I sat down to write and realized I didn't need to instruct or educate. I didn't need to quip. I didn't need to make another list of the best things about x, y, or z. Instead, I needed to tune in to a deeper place—awash with emotion without being swept away. I needed my handwritten words to honor and connect and serve as the long embrace I could not give physically. In short, I needed to write two very different love letters: one to my mother and the other to a neighbor.

Letter to my mother

My mother, who lives in another state, had been having an increasingly difficult couple of years, taking on more and more responsibilities in caring for my mentally ailing father. Finally, in early 2020, she had to move my father into assisted living— with no visitation allowed. This move was utter anguish for her. At the time, though, she was still caring for him and was facing the milestone of turning eighty. I wanted to show her I saw how difficult these past years had been, that I was proud of her, and that she still seemed so young and lively.

My mother, who lived in occupied Holland during World War II, grew up to be passionate about survival stories. I wrote a letter about her love of survival stories as a metaphor for her current difficulties. Her mainsail husband was torn, and the ship of their life was floundering. She faced an endless sea with no guarantee they would find a safe shore together. She relied on strict anti-Alzheimer protocols and supplements like a lost sailor using bare hook lines praying for a nibble of hope. Yet, like that lost sailor appreciating the company of dolphins, she often managed to find something precious to focus on—a new recipe, a cup of tea, a simple walk.

I told her in my love letter what I saw: that the stories of survival she so loved were a pure reflection of her own heart. She harbored little self-pity instead, drawing from a feisty reservoir of inner strength and a deep conviction that she could and would manage whatever life placed before her. She was a survivor and a lover of life, and I wanted her to know that I saw that in her.

It was the most important thing I wrote that year.

I was giving this letter to her, which expressed my love and gratitude while acknowledging her difficult journey, but it also fulfilled me. I felt like I had shown up for her birthday, notwithstanding the distance. Words bridged the gap. Later, she told me receiving the letter meant everything to her and was a turning point in being my dad's caregiver. She relaxed. She was in the middle of a survival story and doing a helluva job. She kept that handwritten card on her kitchen counter and turned to it again and again for solace and comfort.

Not too long after I wrote to my mother, I discovered my neighbor was facing her own life passages. Her husband had died earlier in the year. Shortly after his death, she embarked on a round-the-world journey, then returned home to our neighborhood feeling a little unwell to learn she had inoperable stage IV pancreatic cancer with only months to live.

Letter to a neighbor

In the case of my neighbor, I felt helpless. Imminent death is brutal—not something we, as a culture, are comfortable with. I didn't know what to do or say—even casseroles were not an option. I ran headlong into not being able to "fix" this problem. In facing these truths, I saw that connecting and communicating with someone during difficult times must not require me to fix the problem. Rather, it invited me to radically accept what was in front of me while staying kind, curious, open, and loving. It required me to do my best to connect anyway. To try.

To my neighbor—a woman I did not know well—I sat down one day and gave all my attention to the space she had carved in my heart. I wrote to her about meeting her at yoga and what a deep comfort it was to know that a like-minded soul lived just across the street. I wrote that I appreciated her enthusiastic and engaged approach to life and loved the connection she had with the community and her extended family. I thanked her for the time she went with our daughter to a Zen, Buddha, and the Brain class, even though she was a Christian and the course was far away. I told her I saw her as someone who fit everywhere and made bridges as she went. I mailed it, even though she lived across the street, because her family had indicated she was not accepting visitors, and I appreciated they needed uninterrupted time with her. I wrote it by hand to feel intimate and connected with her.

I needed to draw from a different writing strength to write these letters. My usual communication methods (through a structured essay or three-word lines of encouragement) were inadequate. Instead, I needed to sit quietly, let the words find me,

and allow my writing to flow uninhibited and unstructured—
awash in love while mired in uncertainty. These crucial moments
asked me—a writer—to write not about them so much as from
them—to wade deep in acceptance of the profound difficulties
that life sometimes offers.

Life is full and often sweet, but also precarious and fragile.
It might be happy or sad, messy or clean, perfect or imperfect
at any given moment. We may feel lost and disconnected from
others.

My advice: Take and give solace by writing a love letter and
letting the word tears flow.

Let's practice writing a love letter to another that feels like a
warm embrace.

The practice:

- To write a love letter that feels like a warm embrace, I've
  discovered I must let go of the thinking mind and engage
  the subconscious while tickling the heart. Writing a love
  letter is a "freewriting" exercise for me.
- With one person in mind, follow simple freewriting rules:
  keep the hand moving, don't think, don't edit, don't filter.
  I let it all flow.
- Below are the concepts I consider when writing a love
  letter. I've included them as prompts to get you started.
- Dear _____, I want to write you a letter because...

  ◦ I appreciate that you...
  ◦ You make me feel...
  ◦ I remember when we...
  ◦ Thank you for...
  ◦ I know how hard it has been for you...
  ◦ You are courageous because...

- I guarantee this process will yield tremendous pearls of authentic love you can assemble into a love letter.
- Enjoy the process of putting your letter in an envelope and mailing it! It just might change someone's life.
- Pay attention to your experience in writing your love letter.

Notes: _____

_____

_____

_____

_____

_____

_____

_____

_____

A love letter to yourself

In addition to writing to others, I want to encourage you to also write a love letter to yourself. Similarly, you need to get quiet and sit still for a moment or two, pondering gently in your heart what you appreciate about yourself, noting any difficulties you may have been through recently, and recalling your efforts to overcome them. Think about how hard this precious being has been working to do her best (even when it doesn't feel like enough). We tend to be hardest on ourselves. Sometimes we have to stop and acknowledge all that we have been going through, all we have been doing, and how far we've come. Sometimes it helps to remember delightful moments, so we don't forget them, and to also remember that tough times pass. When we take the time to write to ourselves, we validate our life's ups and downs. In our letter to ourselves, we want to write down what we appreciate, love, and acknowledge what has been challenging.

It helps if we don't think too hard about this, just a freewriting practice as easy as a light breeze.

Here are some prompts to get the juices flowing.

Remember to say, "I love you!"

The practice:

- Try using these prompts to write yourself a love letter:

  ◦ Dear [use a unique nickname for yourself that makes you smile]
  ◦ Do you remember when you... [insert special memory, including small details]
  ◦ I'm sorry that it has been such a hard time lately...
  ◦ I'm proud of you for...
  ◦ What I love about you is...
  ◦ Your most beautiful character flaw is...
  ◦ I honor your...
  ◦ In your heart, I know you...
  ◦ Signed, your... [insert a whimsical phrase that points to your inner guidance]

- Put this in an envelope and label it "To the one who knows my heart." You might even want to snail mail it to yourself, for fun.
- One other fantastic thing to do with a love letter to yourself is to read it aloud and record it (most smartphones have a recording app). It can be profound to hear your voice telling you everything you love and appreciate about yourself, acknowledging any hard times, and honoring the being for doing their best.

Notes: _____

_____

_____

_____

_____

_____

_____

_____

_____

Chapter 8

Communication Tips Unveiled

The single biggest problem in communication is the illusion that it has taken place.

—George Bernard Shaw

In the last chapter, we began investigating some practices that can help us restore or rejuvenate our relationships. I want to take it to the next step and talk about some communication tips that have proven invaluable to me over the years. These tips stem from my experience—flailing my way through hardship, stumbling while trying to communicate with my beloved—but also from my years as a mediator, working to help folks who found themselves on opposite sides of an issue to communicate.

In this chapter, we will lightly touch on a few communication tips. Many books dive deep into communication pitfalls and breakthroughs, especially in the context of relationships. For instance, a friend, Vincentia Schroeder, wrote one you might want to check out: *Communication Breakthrough: How Using Brain Science and Listening to Body Cues Can Transform Your Relationships.*

Please don't assume you will find everything you need to know about communication in this chapter. Instead, allow it to be a springboard to noticing what our tendencies are (typically self-centered) and possibly trying out for yourself different little techniques with the intent to get the playful and juicy back into our sticky conversations.

We'll talk about the simplest form of communication that can immediately act as a bridge: a smile. How learning to listen is, perhaps, our most potent and underappreciated tool in improving our communications. Finally, we'll examine how setting up an intentional sacred space can aid difficult conversations. How remaining curious and open through the art of asking questions opens doors, creates intimacy, and allows you to explore vulnerability with another.

Let's practice!

Practice #19: The Power of a Smile

Before we dive into the meat of this chapter, I want to draw our attention to one of the most basic forms of communication available to us. Smiling is a form of communication that breaks language, culture, gender, and age barriers—freely crossing boundaries. This magic is the power of a smile.

Have you noticed what happens inside when you see someone smile? Next time, watch. Notice the intricate little details that occur when someone smiles at you. There tends to be a softening inside you, a letting go of tension, a dropping of the shoulders. Often smiles are contagious, and when someone smiles at you, you can hardly help but smile back. But have you ever investigated what happens when you smile yourself?

Practicing smiling just for yourself is a meditation technique all to itself. Armed with nothing but the power of your attention to notice what happens when you gently engage a soft inner smile, you can change your attitude in a moment. I encourage you to spend one minute a day simply noticing what happens inside your body and mind when you intentionally engage an inner smile.

Let's investigate this right now, and then you can practice it later.

The practice:

- Close your eyes just now and allow everything to drop. Allow your shoulders and your cheeks to drop. Let your face come to rest. Notice the breath moving through your nostrils, expanding the belly.
- Now. Activate a slight inner "Mona Lisa" smile and pay close attention to what happens when you do. A little air of possibility enters as the cheekbones lift ever so slightly.

There is a light feeling in the face as if it were upturned to the sun, taking in warm rays for the sheer pleasure of it.

- Now, let your cheeks fall again and watch what happens. There may be calm, but sometimes also a slight heaviness returns. Engage the inner smile and notice the warmth that spreads across the face and chest from nothing more than this ever-so-slight inner smile.

- Practice adding your eyes into your slight inner smile. What happens when you allow your inner smile to reach your eyes? What thoughts are triggered? When I let a smile include my eyes, such that they twinkle a little, I feel happy—notwithstanding anything else.

- This little inner smile is your secret weapon. When you don't know what else to do. Take one minute out and play with the effect of a smile—one that is just for you.

- Then take your smile on the road. Notice how relaxing it is to smile at another person. Especially in this day and age when masks have deprived us of the joy of smiling at each other, use your smile widely and often. If you still are wearing a mask, go ahead and smile bigger; let it reach your eyes so that you and another can share a simple moment of peace and happiness.

- What does it feel like to arm yourself with a smile?

Notes: _____

_____

_____

_____

_____

_____

_____

_____

Practice #20: The Art of Listening Reflectively

I mentioned above that the tips I share in this chapter come from my personal experience. Some were things taught to me during mediation classes, and some I discovered for myself that I later read about more. For example, as I got curious about communication, what made it flow, and what made it get stuck, I began to notice that when communication flowed, I felt happier. In contrast, when it did not, I felt unhappy, and the difference hinged on my desire to be heard and understood.

I noticed both in my interactions and in facilitating the mediations of others that when we are having trouble communicating with someone, it is because we feel unheard. We seek to explain our side so that the other person "understands" our point of view. As the gap widens, our efforts take on an urgency and seriousness. We speak louder, sharper, more forcefully. Instead of getting closer, we seem to get entrenched in our positions. As the gap grows wider, getting the other to see our point of view feels of utmost importance to moving forward. *How can I communicate with another if they cannot hear what I am saying?*

That's how it was with me.

Though we deeply love each other, my husband and I have had a difficult time communicating at various times in our long relationship. Where previously we had easily exchanged sweet nothings or felt safe enough to risk being vulnerable and share deeply held secrets, at other times, we would find ourselves at odds with one another, unable to communicate at all. At those times, I wanted him to understand how I felt—sure that once he understood how I felt (and the irrefutable logic behind my words), he would see things my way—of course he would.

If I can just explain myself better, he'll see things my way; he loves me, right? We are close, right?

This inner narrative was the loop stuck in my head. I would come at the issue from subtly different perspectives, all to get him to understand my point of view. I would even focus on telling him how I felt, utilizing the therapist's tools of saying "I feel..." instead of pointing and blaming. Still, the conversation often did not unfold as I thought it would in my head. Instead (from my point of view), he would become obstreperous. The more I sought to have him understand me, the more entrenched we would become.

I missed our "sweet nothing" talks and being vulnerable. I wanted to be heard, but I also missed the sound of his voice—the particular timbre and resonance it has when he quietly shares something with me. I missed his presence even though he was right there. Then, one day, I realized that I was not hearing him— both figuratively and literally—that I had become so interested in being heard that I had forgotten to listen. Though I thought I had experienced that he was not present for me, it was equally valid that I was not present for him. At that moment, everything turned around as I realized that he wanted what I wanted: to be heard. I realized that to reconnect with him (a new goal instead of being heard), I had to practice listening.

At that point, our relationship was shaky. We had developed bad habits, wherein we each were self-centered, wanting to be right—wanting the other person to see things our way. In addition, we had begun to fear talking with each other because we were sure the other would not hear us anyway.

Motivated by missing our connection, I privately (unbeknownst to him) began to change my focus. Internally, instead of focusing on how to make my point better, I began to wonder, *What is he trying to say? What am I not hearing? How can I be more present while he is speaking? What if I listen, not only to the words but the spaces between the words and to his timbre? What if I listened with all my heart to him?* I didn't know it at the time, but this was the beginning of learning how to be an active listener.

The truth is communication is complex. Words often fail to capture what we are feeling. There are many barriers; word choices can cause embittered arguments when a particular term means one thing to one person and something else to another. Letting go of an urgent need to be heard and replacing it with a sincere desire to hear is not easy.

As I embarked on my new goal—learning how to listen—I noticed that I had to talk a *lot* less to hear what he was saying. I had to change my focus from where my mind wanted to line up its subsequent arguments, aching to make a point, to where I waited with bated breath to see what he would say next. I noticed that he processed his feelings much slower than I did. If pushed too quickly, he blurted anything out in defense—not because those were his most exact words but because he hadn't fully processed his feelings yet. He needed much more quiet time to sort through things.

A change happened inside me as we readied for bed. Instead of filling that quiet space with my words, I allowed there to be some quiet. Instead of dreading the exchange where I broached a subject anticipating my husband would not see things my way, I waited, hoping that he would open his mouth and speak first. Many nights we went to bed quietly, and there were no words. He had often said that nighttime (which always seemed like the perfect time for me to talk) was not a good time for him. He was tired and not up for an extensive discussion. I had noticed, though, that when there was a bit of silence in the air without any expectation of an ensuing discussion—a pregnant pause, where I was not speaking but was available and alert—he would begin speaking. And the words that eventually came out were thoughtful, considered, fascinating, and revealing. I would lay in bed each night like a cat at a mousehole, wondering if he would speak and what those words might be. This new private practice of learning how to listen became one of my life's most essential and personal lessons.

Sometimes we stumble onto these lessons, all the sweeter for having discovered them ourselves, but there is plenty of research behind them. A quick Google search on "kinds of listening" will bring forth a slew of articles about all the different kinds of listening there are, Some say there are three types; some say four, others seven. For now, I am focusing on what I call active listening. Active listening seeks to connect rather than to evaluate, analyze, or judge. I realized that to reconnect with my husband and improve communication, I needed to learn how to listen actively. I had to focus on the speaker and my intent to understand, not just respond. And to do this, I had to interrupt my brain's habit of taking mental shortcuts and instantly trying to formulate a response, defense, or argument while he was speaking. I had to change my focus from making a point or being "right" to understanding what was going on with him.

If it is closeness with another we seek, a tendency to take quick mental shortcuts and strive to be "right" can lead us astray. We might misinterpret what is going on. As a result, we might miss clues that our beloved needs empathy.

Imagine a spouse walks into the house after a long, difficult day at work, beat, looking forward to relaxing at home. Instead, the house smells funky, and the trash is overflowing. An immediate feeling of overwhelm sets in, and all they think to say at that moment, perhaps somewhat accusingly, is: "You didn't take out the trash! It's rotting and the kitchen smells terrible!"

The other suddenly feels defensive and unappreciated and yells back, glaring: "I've been driving the kids around all day, and the dog threw up! You can take out the trash. Who made it my job anyway?"

And the conversation devolves into whose job it is to take out the trash. It seems like one or the other is upset about the trash, but with just a little digging, it is clear there is a bigger issue. Often, the first thing we think to say is *not* the heart of the matter, hence the saying by Eckhart Tolle (also found in *A Course in Miracles*): "I am never upset for the reason I think."

Though the initial words out of the working spouse's mouth sounded accusing, the issue was not about the trash. Instead, it was about already feeling overwhelmed and needing a calm, supportive environment to relax and regroup.

I posit that often we are upset, not so much because they didn't take out the trash (which may have come to signify to us they don't care about us) but because we lost our connection with one another. (Have you ever heard the saying "You can be right, or you can be happy"? It points to our brain's tendency to conclude the "right" way something should go, based solely on our perspective. But of course, the catch is that tendency is not optimizing us to feel inner peace or happiness.)

I had to learn how to interrupt that process to reconnect and communicate more deeply with my husband.

Psychology often calls this "active" listening or mindful listening. It relies on all the skills we have been learning thus far to help us get naked in the now: it requires us, first and foremost, to be present and self-aware. We must decide to devote our attention to the speaker instead of our own thoughts and practice non-judgment. Remember this is a practice! (A particularly juicy one at that.) We don't have to be perfect at it immediately. We will get ample opportunity to try again. But it is a choice—a different way of approaching a conversation. We notice and observe our thoughts in the background but return our attention repeatedly to the speaker. Plus, we allow there to be bits of silence, little pauses in between the words.

We don't typically learn to listen and allow spaces between words in conversation. The family communication dynamics I grew up with involved interrupting each other and talking over one another—not necessarily with evil intent, often heartily and in the spirit of lively conversation—but without gaps. Nor is it modeled much in society. We value banter and quick-wittedness. We fear not being heard so much that we learn to talk louder, to yell to get our point across. We practice formulating what to say next while another is speaking.

But at some point in our relations with another, we might realize that connecting with them is more important than making a point (and I propose that in our intimate relationships, it often is). So, what can we do instead of racing to protect our point of view? We can stop and listen—really listen.

When I stumbled onto this on my own, I recognized that I needed to practice being quiet, to listen to others. To do so, I needed to unlearn my tendency to respond to defend myself quickly. Instead, I needed to stop and pay attention, alert to what my beloved said and all the other cues presented. I needed to allow space between their words and mine to let the silence speak as much as the words.

Later, I improved my listening skills further, and in addition to staying quiet and alert, I learned the fine art of reflective listening, an extension of active listening.

Reflective listening is like magic. We practice it by paraphrasing or summarizing slightly what someone has said and repeating it back to them. It even works if you use their exact words.

Why does this work so well? Because when we do this, we indicate that we did hear what someone was saying, and the result is they felt heard. When someone feels heard, the tension drips away.

Getting to the heart of the matter—or, as I think, back to juicy—needs a little space and requires us to practice both active and reflective listening. Listening has become one of my own most essential tenets. So, when asked to distill my motto for living an enlivened and juicy life, it came down to this: Listen. Play. Write.

I recently learned of a famous international speaker and sound expert, Julian Treasure. He says we are losing our hearing. We live in a noisy world and have almost lost the ability to listen to each other. He is on a mission to teach all of us how to listen. I listened to his TED Talk, "5 Ways to Listen Better," and immediately found him to be a kindred spirit. He succinctly talked about what I had discovered on my own: learn to listen to silence, practice sensory awakening (listening to discrete sounds), and practice active listening. In addition, he has a beautiful acronym about how to listen that I'd like to share: RASA. The acronym tickles me because it means "juice" or essence in Sanskrit.

So, all you juicy practitioners out there, come along with me and practice RASA:

R — receive
A — appreciate (make little noises indicating you have heard)
S — summarize
A — ask

What might this look like in real life?

Consider the trash example above. Imagine that all the conditions are the same. We have the working spouse and the home spouse. The working spouse comes home feeling overwhelmed because their project has a significant problem, and their boss is upset with them. They walk into a house with an overflowing trash can and a stinking kitchen. They immediately lash out at the spouse at home who, in their opinion, could or should have taken out the trash because *it's rotting for criminy sake, and they were home.*

Working spouse says: "You didn't take out the trash. It's rotting and the kitchen smells terrible! I can't take this. I'm tired."

The home spouse, at this moment, has a choice. They can lash out, defending themselves about their kid duties and the dog barf (they have feelings too, after all), or they can pause and recognize this moment as an opportunity to give their spouse full attention. They can notice all the nonverbal cues that accompany words.

So, in this new example, the home spouse pauses, allowing a little space in, and maybe breathes deep into the belly to help stabilize their attention because their brain is screaming inside: *Oh my god! They are talking about the trash! They have no idea how hard this day was! Why is it* my *job to take out the trash?*

But instead of speaking these words, they sit down and look directly at their partner (Receive), noticing fatigue etching their face, and nod a little murmuring agreement (Appreciate). "You look wiped out."

Then, after a bit says, "You noticed I didn't take out the trash. You can smell it in the kitchen and it feels overwhelming and not relaxing." (Summarize)

Pause.

"Sounds like you had a tough day. Do you want to tell me about it?" (Ask)

Of course, there are different ways this conversation might flow at that point, but sometimes it's helpful to let go of our desire to be heard and instead seek to understand. Julian Treasure says, "Listening is our access to understanding," and "We must listen consciously to live fully."

Getting to the heart of the matter—the *juicy, naked now*—needs a little space and requires us to practice better active listening skills. The practice below may be the biggest game-changer of all!

The practice:

- Remember the acronym RASA for reflective listening:

Receive
Appreciate
Summarize
Ask

- The next time your partner shares anything with you, particularly something emotional or troublesome, practice reflective listening. (Your partner needn't even know you are practicing.)
- Show attentiveness. You can use body language, such as leaning forward and maintaining eye contact, showing that you are paying attention. You can also murmur little sounds, nod, or say, "Go on..." or "I'm listening." Again, be quietly attentive until there is silence at the end.
- When there is a break in what they say, or it seems they are looking for feedback, start by mirroring or paraphrasing what you heard them say.
- You can use phrases to help you get started:
  - It sounds like you...
  - What I'm hearing is...
  - I can see that you are feeling...
  - Can you tell me more about...?
- Also, pay attention to how they feel, even if they don't say it in words. We often have a sense, and accurately noticing and describing their feelings to them shows empathy, engendering trust.
- You can use phrases like the following to help you get started:
  - So, you feel...

- ○ I can see you are feeling...
- ○ It can be frustrating when someone misunderstands us...
- Finally, you can ask follow-up questions to confirm what you learned from them:
  - ○ Did I get that right?
  - ○ Is that correct?
  - ○ Can you tell me more about...?

Notes: _____

_____

_____

_____

_____

_____

_____

_____

_____

Practice #21: How to Have Hard Conversations

Later on, in Chapter 10, "Getting Naked," we will talk about how to set up a sacred space as a first step in opening a channel for the trust that allows increased vulnerability. The idea behind setting up a sacred space is to set an intention to move from our usual way of interacting into something else—something more intentional done with awareness and attention. This ritual can be profoundly helpful for working on intimacy, but the principles can also help us enter into any "hard" conversation.

To create the "sacred space" equivalent for tricky communications with someone other than our lover, we still need to signal to ourselves that we are ready to be attentive listeners or have created an environment conducive to someone else being an attentive listener.

Pre-communication stage

In her workshop entitled Effective Communication: How to Have a Hard Conversation, Sanni Honnold calls this the critical "pre-communication stage." Sanni (featured in the movie *Free Solo*) is the co-founder of Outwild—an event series focusing on community and life design for the outdoor-minded. She is a beloved and sought-after life coach from whom I have learned a lot. She is also my daughter.

Sanni counsels that in the pre-communication stage we need to ready ourselves and the other to have a hard conversation. Much like working together to co-create a sacred space is beneficial, getting someone to participate in the idea of having a hard conversation is immensely helpful.

In my years as a mediator, I greatly appreciated this stage. When two parties in the middle of a distressing conflict agree to mediate, there is already a meeting ground for the simple fact that there is a mutual desire to talk.

To start, a day or two beforehand, give the other person a heads-up and let the person know you would like to talk to them about a subject that has been tricky in the past. This advance notice helps the other person be emotionally prepared and willing to go into the conversation. If you are juggling tight schedules, or even if you are not, it can help to set a time and place for the discussion. Consider also the space. It can be helpful to meet in a different room or area than expected.

Then, before you jump into the meat of the issue, take the time to set the tone—this is the lover equivalent of hanging twinkle lights—to create an atmosphere of collaboration and understanding.

Your words might differ depending on whether this hard conversation is with a partner, friend, or work colleague. However, you still want to acknowledge the difficulties of the past or whatever difficulties you are aware of the other one going through, and comment on the topic of discussion and the potential upside for both of you if you engage in the conversation.

I have wanted people to "tell me the words" to use, and Sanni has said that her clients often ask her the same thing. For that reason, I've included (with her permission) some sample scripts culled from Sanni Honnold's Four Steps for Having Effective Communication.

These are from step one, pre-communication:

Example with a partner and a topic that you frequently bicker about

I know when we've talked about this in the past we've both gotten angry and felt attacked. I hope today we can talk about this from a place of love. I know it's important to both of us that this issue gets resolved.

Example with a friend who hurt your feelings

This is by no means the end of our friendship and I'm not trying to attack you, I just wanted to let you know about something that hurt my feelings. I know you care about me and did not mean to hurt me which is why I hope bringing it up will help.

Example with a boss when you're asking for something

I know you have a lot on your plate and things have been hectic around the office. I wanted to talk to you about something that I feel could help me work more effectively and therefore make things easier on our whole team.

As you go into a challenging conversation, some other tips can help you too. It sounds obvious, but it helps to remember hard conversations are hard. Even as we practice using tools for improving communication, things might get sticky. For this reason, it helps to acknowledge this within yourself from the start. It's not that we should expect things to go awry, but at some point, you or the other person will likely feel uncomfortable during this conversation.

If you set the expectation that since you took all the proper steps to have this communication it shouldn't feel uncomfortable, you can set yourself up for failure. Things can quickly go sideways as soon as the other person does not respond in the way we want. For that reason, the next tip I have for you is to be willing to be uncomfortable.

Willingness to be uncomfortable

The first time I learned this was when Sanni was about thirteen. She had just started getting interested in boys, and I noticed she shut her computer down whenever I came near. This behavior happened during the early era of instant messenger.

I wanted to talk to her about it and warn her about internet stalkers. We had always had a close and easy relationship. But the one or two times I tried, I suddenly found the air between us sticky and uncomfortable. She looked defensive and clammed up.

I talked to my friend Durga, a meditation teacher, who said this one simple sentence that changed everything.

"What's wrong with being uncomfortable?" she said.

I pondered that and realized that I was afraid of the feeling of discomfort. I expected my conversation with my daughter to unfold seamlessly as it always had; I wanted to give up when it didn't. But that left me feeling helpless and frustrated, not to mention worried.

So, at the next available opportunity, I broached the subject again. As expected, the air got sticky, and she got an angry look. Then, she shut down and wouldn't say anything, making me even more worried. In past attempts, I would have walked away or possibly pushed her for a response — neither of which worked.

This time, instead, I just stood there armed only with the idea that this conversation was going to be uncomfortable — that I was going to feel uncomfortable — and that was okay.

In silence, discomfort notwithstanding, just remaining present had an unexpected result. Eventually, my daughter turned to me and said, "It's just a guy from school. He reaches out on instant messenger to me sometimes. We're just friends."

Immediately I relaxed. We were talking, and now I better understood what this was about.

I told her I understood her wanting to be private about some relationships but that I also wanted her to know that boys were bound to be an essential part of her life and that I hoped I could get to know them, just as I had her girlfriends. Then we talked about how important it was to only connect with people you know personally.

"You're not mad?" she asked.

"No," I replied. "Would you like to invite him over? I would love to meet him."

And with that, the energy shifted. She became almost chatty about her new friend. Thus, we began a new era together. And, I had learned an important lesson. Being willing to be uncomfortable is part of the process when we grow, change, and learn how to have hard conversations with one another.

Gaps between the words — the power of silence

In the example above, I mentioned that I had to stand in silence, attentive but not speaking, while I allowed my daughter time to process her feelings and to find her way forward to talk about a boy who had recently come into her life.

Silence can be a critical component of having a hard conversation. But unfortunately, we are not trained to allow silence in our discussions. Instead, we rush to explain our point of view, offer our expertise or wit, or point a blaming finger. But hard conversations need something else altogether. They need us to be present and attentive to one another, listening carefully.

If we didn't have differing opinions or weren't afraid or worried, we wouldn't be broaching a challenging conversation in the first place. Silence is an under-used tool in conversation, but gaps between thoughts allow a more authentic, more considered response to arise — not the first thing we want to speak out to protect our position, but something more profound and closer to the truth of the issue. We must be willing to sit in our judgment without acting on it.

In the example above, my brain was screaming as I stood in silence. Oh no! Something is wrong. Sanni is shutting her computer down because she knows she is participating in risky behavior. Sanni is going to be taken advantage of by an internet predator who has used his wiles to hook up with her. I need to protect her. I need her to stop immediately. I need to forbid her to interact online with this person!

And, while all of that could have been true, I couldn't know without talking to her. And I had already witnessed what happened when I pushed; she contracted and refused to talk about it. So, I needed to employ a new technique: sit in the uncomfortable silence with her while my inner thoughts were screaming *danger*, and allow her the chance to decide what to say.

I encourage you to practice adding silence into your conversations—little gaps between when someone else speaks and you speak. My husband and I have been participating in a mid-week meeting with a collection of friends we met at a Quaker group. Each week we read and discuss a piece of literature or poetry. The only rule in our interaction together is that nobody is allowed to interrupt another. And to be clear, if someone starts talking and doesn't yield for a while, we listen and wait for that person to come to a complete stop. Wow. It takes practice to not step over the words of another, not to rush to tell your piece, and to allow silence as much as speaking to direct a conversation. It takes practice to let each person fully explain their side or perspective without rushing in too quickly with our own. These weekly meetings have taught me more about authentic communication than any other tool in my life. Now, I pay attention to different situations and practice letting other people speak. I fail a lot, but that practice has also been fruitful over the years. I talk much less than I used to. It feels good.

And while hard conversations are not "negotiations" per se, it helps to note that silence has long been a powerful tool in negotiations. Not only might the other side reveal critical information during the silence, but you can learn a lot about what might appeal to the one you are negotiating with. Moreover, this style of dealing (with lots of listening and gaps between speaking) helps build trust and earn respect.

Finally, while we don't typically allow silence in our conversations, we do sometimes wield silence as a weapon of sorts. We do this when we are being passively aggressive with another. For example, when we are mad, we may employ the silent treatment as a punishment for the other person. I am *not* talking about this kind of silence, where we contract, turn our face away from the other, and refuse to say anything because they don't deserve our words. I am talking about intentional attentive silence.

A third-party facilitator

Sometimes, the most helpful path forward is to employ the help of a third-party facilitator. This person might be a therapist or a mediator—someone trained in helping two opposing sides speak their truth so that each side really hears the other and works in collaboration to resolve an issue. (Interestingly, if you are in an argument with your own self, a life coach can help you sort out your own thoughts so that you can listen to each part of your own self.)

After working in the legal industry as a freelance paralegal for fifteen years I became interested in mediation. I had seen multi-million-dollar construction defect cases get resolved amicably during mediation—a solution that seemed vastly superior to everyone pointing fingers and spending millions on legal defense. It resonated with something deep inside me and it no longer felt in integrity to help litigate cases.

In 2003, against the odds, I became a certified mediator in North Carolina, one of only a handful of non-attorney mediators in the state allowed to work with the courts. I volunteered for the District Criminal Court Mediation program in Durham, North Carolina, worked for the child custody and visitation mediation program and a community center, and started a business mediating superior court cases.

I was interested in mediation for the unexpected resolutions that came about—resolutions that often ended up with life-changing results. However, one case stands out above the others, illustrating the benefit of resolving conflict through mediation.

A mom was about to sue her neighbor for an egregious peace disturbance. The situation was this: She was the mother of a sick three- or four-year-old girl. The girl was ailing in some way and needed to take afternoon naps, but each afternoon, just as the little girl went down for a rest, the new neighbors' (who lived kitty-corner behind them) dogs began barking. The barking was so loud and went on for so long that the little girl could not sleep. The little girl loved dogs, and the barking dogs made her more awake, not less. Unfortunately, she was allergic to dogs, and they could not get their own. The mom had tried asking that the neighbors keep the dogs in the house at least, desperate for her girl to get her nap, but they refused, saying they would try to get home to walk them.

I listened to the mom's story about her sick child and empathized with her. It seemed reasonable that the people with the dogs should have to keep them under control. Then I listened to the story of the young couple.

The young couple had bought their first starter home, excited that it had a backyard for their beloved dogs. But they both had taken on new jobs to pay for the home. They walked the dogs in the morning before going to work and tried to get home midday to walk the dogs (which always made the dogs settle down for the afternoon), but with the demands of new jobs and a commute, they often couldn't make it. They were happy that their dogs at least had a yard to play in and felt bad when they couldn't make it home at lunch to walk them, but what were they supposed to do? Get rid of their dogs? Move? Their dogs were family. I felt empathy for this young couple, who loved their pets and were not bad, neglectful dog owners but rather did their best under the circumstances.

When they had a chance to fully tell their story, in such a way that the mom could see what kind of people they were, something softened in the mom. We began brainstorming ideas together. Although their finances were tight, the couple said maybe they could hire a dog walker to come to the house. This solution would be excellent for their dogs, too.

Suddenly, a lightbulb went off in the mom's head, and she slowly turned to the couple and said, "Wait a minute! I have an idea. My daughter loves dogs and regularly begs me to get one, but we can't because she is allergic and it will further compromise her. But what if she and I became your dog walkers? We could come over each afternoon and take the dogs for a walk. This would serve multiple purposes," she said excitedly as the idea took hold. "My daughter would get to develop a relationship with dogs that didn't have to live with us. The dogs would get a walk and my daughter, too, which will help all of them settle down better in the afternoon."

We all looked at each other in shock at the brilliant simplicity of the solution. The young couple was hesitantly ecstatic. "Really? Really, you might be interested in doing that? We would love for our dogs to have some company during the day! We have felt awful about leaving them for too long and have thought about quitting our jobs and moving. But this, this solution would be amazing!"

Later the mom contacted me and told me the solution worked out perfectly. Everyone was happy, and she was great friends with the young couple now, and her daughter was thrilled to have two animal friends in her life.

The practice:
Let's review our simple communication tips.

- **Pre-communication stage**
  - Get the other ready and willing to participate in a hard conversation.
  - Set a date and time and think about how to set the tone for the conversation.
  - For lovers seeking more intimacy, this might include setting up a "sacred space" (see Chapter 10).

- **Willingness to be uncomfortable**
  - Remember hard conversations often make us feel uncomfortable at first and that's okay.

- **Gaps between the words — the power of silence**
  - Practice not interrupting and allowing silence to guide the conversation as well as words.

- **Third-party facilitator**
  - Consider using a third-party facilitator to help each side fully be heard and to help the two parties brainstorm creative solutions.

Notes: _____

_____

_____

_____

_____

_____

_____

_____

_____

Chapter 9

The Power of Presence

Presence is the felt sense of your subtle body being available and open and aware. There's a silence to it as well, because presence has a quiet quality to it.
— Adyashanti, *The Direct Way*

As children (and lovers), we know the power of someone's attention—of their presence. We seek it out, hoping that our parents (or our beloved) will slow down enough to be only with us, to connect and play undistracted with us. We know, too, what it feels like when it is missing. And when it is, we thrash about, act out, and demand attention, so badly are we hoping that someone else will be present with us.

But what is presence? What is it that we are seeking?

Let's investigate.

First, it seems evident that being present with someone is related to where we are directing our attention. Any child (or cat) knows that when Mom or Dad is talking on the phone or working at the computer, for instance, he or she is not paying attention to them—is not present with them even if there are intermittent smiles and murmurs of affection their way. So, from a cognitive point of view, being present requires us to direct our undistracted attention.

But this is only part of it, for we are not just a thinking mind but also a feeling, sensing body. The experience of presence is more than a mind trick; it is an embodied phenomenon—a sudden and distinct realization of being alive at this moment, not waiting for something else. There is a transformative shift when we both direct our attention and allow ourselves to relax into our sensing body simultaneously. What happens when we do? The California Institute of Integral Studies puts it this way: "When you are deeply present with others, there is a communion that goes beyond words—a felt connection that touches, enlivens, and inspires."

When we are present, there is a *felt* sense of being in this body, at this moment right now, attentive and connected without resistance. It is the quintessential essence of being naked in the now.

Being present is daring work, for it calls for us to unabashedly allow whatever is arising without flinching, rushing to quell, and hurrying to the next thing. Instead, it calls for us to direct our attention to right here, right now, while feeling ourselves in this body—not disassociated, not distracted.

Maybe we think we can't do that. Perhaps that sounds hard or scary. Maybe we fear that terrible thoughts or overwhelming feelings will arise if we stop doing and sit still. Maybe we feel like we don't have the time to do that.

But here's the thing, as we practice sitting for even brief moments of embodied attentive silence, we learn that we can do this. We can be present at the drop of a hat effortlessly. Presence is readily available at any moment. And it feels delicious.

Simple presence is what we are all genuinely seeking deep down inside.

I say "simple" intentionally. It may not be easy at first, and we may stumble; learning to walk does not necessarily come instantly with ease. But similarly, all it requires is willingness and practice: stand up, find your balance, and put one foot in front of the other.

In this chapter, I want you to taste how simple dipping into embodied presence, alone and with another, can be. We will start with a five-second practice you can do at any time during the day. These five seconds offer us a window to a tiny, vibrantly alive moment—like standing and getting our balance, feeling pure potential as we lean forward to take a step with curiosity but not urgency. Then we will take some steps and practice sustained beingness with ourselves and others with this same quality of presence.

Practice #22: Five Seconds of Presence

Let's start with something we can practice at any moment. It only takes five seconds and it reminds us to tune into the tangible, physical sense of being.

The practice:

- Stop.
- Right now.
- Be still.
- Open all your senses and turn your attention to the *felt* sense of being.

Can you feel it?
There is a subtle undercurrent always present anytime we stop and tune in to it. Some call it an energetic body or embodied presence. Unlike the sharp pain of a particular body sensation such as a sore back or injured knee, this felt sense of being hovers around and through the body, invisible and diffuse but visceral.

- Close your eyes for a moment to decrease visual distractions.
- Look for it now, in the quiet stillness of your own body, at this moment.
- Can you feel that subtle kinesthetic sense of *aliveness* rooted in the experience of being present in the body?
- It is that subtle, kinesthetic sense of aliveness rooted in the experience of being present in the body that we want to tune in to.
- Enlivenment, love, and clarity live here. And, it is available to us *anytime*.

- Just five seconds.
- That's all we need to experience this visceral sense of presence directly.
- The visceral sense of presence described above is the backdrop to another couple of powerful practices we will discuss in this chapter: soul gazing and mirror meditation. The first you do with another, the latter with yourself. These exercises allow us to experience the power of presence beyond five seconds while thoughts and feelings about others or ourselves are simmering below the surface. Don't forget to take notes!

Notes: _____

_____

_____

_____

_____

_____

_____

_____

Practice #23: Soul Gazing

It's been twenty-five years since my husband, Jay, and I learned to soul gaze. Yet, it is something we still practice every day.

We first learned the technique at an introductory love and ecstasy workshop that we took after he had an affair. The affair had spurred me to question everything I thought I knew to be true about life, about us.

After some initial soul searching, followed by couple's therapy where I had to acknowledge my role in the breakdown of our relationship, we chose not to separate. Instead, we decided to dive deeper into ourselves and each other. We learned to meditate and began studying sacred sexuality together.

We ended up taking a yearlong Love and Ecstasy Training with Margo Anand (author of *The Art of Sexual Ecstasy*) that taught us and gave us ample opportunity to practice different meditation and self-inquiry techniques: how to heal invisible wounds, how to be vulnerable with one another, how to be playful, how to let the other in, and how to communicate our wants and needs.

But even before we benefitted from all the training of the yearlong class, we took that initial introductory weekend workshop with Margo Anand and learned how to soul gaze.

Soul gazing is not something we are typically trained to do in our society, and when we first tried it, it felt uncomfortable but tickled something inside.

Soul gazing is essentially a reciprocated invitation to be present with each other—not escaping, disassociated, hiding or averting, or blaming, just sitting looking deeply into each other's eyes. It feels extraordinarily vulnerable and incredibly intimate.

At that initial workshop, as I sat across from this man to whom I had been married for eleven years, I worried, what does he see in my eyes? Does he see my insecurities? My shame? Does he see my righteousness and blaming? Anger or sadness?

"Too invasive!" trilled my mind, but I kept looking and what I saw reflected in his eyes was a steady, unwavering presence.

What occurred then was that maybe we were after the same thing after all — we just hadn't known how to find it.

For us, soul gazing opened a door we didn't even know was shut. More than the passion that typically fuels an intimate encounter, soul gazing encourages the couple to be still, to allow emotions to arise and pass away while remaining simply present.

I think of soul gazing as a portal to the present moment — a shared, timeless moment where boundaries soften and stillness pervades.

Soul gazing is a concentration meditation with your partner's eyes serving as the meditation object instead of the breath or mantra. It requires a little persistence to get the hang of.

Even now, so many years later, when we relax opposite each other looking into each other's eyes, an invisible veil first separates us. His constricted pupils reflect swirling thoughts mirroring my own. Worry, past baggage, and to-do lists clamor for my attention, but... then there is something more compelling.

I feel the seduction of his gaze, lulling me like a soft kiss leaving me intrigued and curious. I soften my gaze, relaxing, opening. I stop looking for anything — stop classifying and analyzing to receive him.

I watch as his pupils widen slightly. I breathe deeper, nostrils flaring, letting in more of him, more of life. I let go of thinking and judging and allow connection. I focus on one of his eyes only and soften my gaze, relaxing into my heart, vulnerable and open.

His gaze penetrates me the same way a kiss becomes passionate, crosses boundaries, invades privacy, and is welcome.

I feel our energies comingle as in an Alex Grey painting, an auric bubble of awareness encompassing two souls as one.

We sit gazing. Just being together, not doing. Then, my peripheral vision finally begins to fade—his face morphs in shadows. Time stops.

Who is he? Who am I?

And then, he is me, and I him. His eyes reflect the whole universe, and I feel that within myself too.

The practice:

- Begin in a seated position facing each other, wherever you feel comfortable, on the floor, in bed, or on chairs.
- Offer a Heart Salutation to each other (hands in prayer position at the chest and bowing).
- Touch your partner in a relaxing way, maybe lightly holding hands.
- Close your eyes and take a moment to go inward. Notice if your mind is distracted with thoughts about the day, such as your to-do list. Gently bring your attention away from those thoughts to your breath for a few moments. Wiggle your shoulders and neck, encouraging the body to relax anywhere that feels tense.
- Take a moment to notice what you are feeling. Tune into your heart and chest area. Do you feel relaxed? Happy? Nervous? If you feel uncomfortable, can you allow yourself to be okay with that?
- Notice any conversations still happening in your mind. Accept them, even as you return your attention to your breath moving through your body.
- Now, try smiling softly to yourself, allowing the corners of your mouth to rise slightly. Notice how that makes you feel.

- When ready, give a small signal to your partner, maybe lightly squeezing their hand. Slowly open your eyes. Allow your gaze to connect.
- Look into one eye of your partner. Quickly choose one (either the left or right) and don't waffle during the exercise. Traditionally, this would be the left eye—the receptive eye. In the Taoist tradition, the left side is Yin, feminine and receptive, while the right is Yang, masculine and active. You might start with the left eye, but if you are naturally drawn to the right eye instead, that's fine. Different sides of our face can hold emotions differently. One eye might look "sadder," "bolder," or "more distant" than the other. Just notice.
- Direct your attention entirely to your gaze.
- Silently say, "We are one," while feeling open to receiving your partner's love.
- Keep your gaze still. The stillness of your gaze helps quiet your mind. As the mind quiets, notice how the Story of I loosens. You cease to identify as strongly with your body, mind, and thoughts and instead become a centered witness.
- Instead of using your eyes to project energy out, analyzing the world at large, do the opposite.

Engage in a great "allowing":

- Allow yourself to open and feel drawn into the innocence of the moment.
- Allow your peripheral vision to soften.
- Allow your eyes to attract energy and love.
- Allow yourself to receive.
- Allow any minor hallucinations, such as distortions of your partner's face or shadows in the room, to be present.

- Allow the breath to move freely.
- Allow a merging—an integration—between seeing, thinking, breathing, and being.
- Allow a feeling of devotion and reverence to be present.
- Let yourself experience your partner beyond their personality. See in your partner the essential humanness that is also present in yourself, and enjoy being present in a mutual flow of breathing, looking, and being without any goal.
- You may gently, without effort, begin to harmonize your breathing with your partner's.
- Notice if you feel it is possible to forgive your partner for any wounds you have been hanging on to. If not, accept that too. All is okay.
- End with a Heart Salutation and the words "I honor you as an aspect of myself."

Notes: _____

_____

_____

_____

_____

_____

_____

_____

_____

Practice #24: Mirror Meditation

I found the mirror was a great way to work out my emotions, too. When I was struggling with negative feelings and there was no one who could lend a compassionate ear—or I just didn't want to upset anyone or say something I'd regret—the mirror became a powerful reflector of my own pain and suffering.
—Tara Well, PhD

That soul-gazing practice is pretty incredible. But what if you do not have a partner with whom to practice soul gazing? No worries. Mirror meditation is the corollary exercise where you don't need anybody else and still have the opportunity to experience something quite similar. All you need is a mirror and a willingness to be still and present.

This powerful exercise is one you can do with yourself to boost self-kindness and self-compassion. It teaches us to accept ourselves exactly as we find ourselves now.

When we first begin practicing this, it might feel difficult and unnatural, for we tend to think about this exercise differently from how we will use it here. For instance, you might think that it sounds narcissistic. But I promise you, it is, as Tara Wells (who teaches mirror meditation) puts it: "Quite the opposite: you'll learn to stay present with yourself, manage the intensity of your emotions, and tap into a new inner strength."

This exercise is not about judging our appearance or imagining how we look to others. Instead, it is about acknowledging ourselves and getting in touch with how we feel. Ultimately, it's about delving beyond the surface of appearance to see deeper into our own eyes with non-judgmental compassion combined with an intrinsic aliveness in our body that is present beneath the thoughts and feelings running through our minds.

It's good to remember that we are each the only person who can consistently be there for ourselves, yet we rarely practice being present with and kind to ourselves. Instead, we focus on how to "fix" ourselves and "improve" ourselves, imagining a future date when we will be better, more deserving, and worthier. But presence does not care whether we have lost or gained weight to improve our appearance, whether we have mastered anger management, or whether we should cry less or laugh more. Presence doesn't care if we feel sad or hopeless or joyful or optimistic. The only thing that matters is whatever is present right now—precisely as it is.

So, we practice. We practice getting used to stopping and accepting ourselves at this moment by looking at our flawed (or perfect) reflection and holding our own attention, allowing our sensing body to be open, noticing all the different emotions, thoughts, and judgments that arise—just noticing. And also, paying attention to the ever-present, bare-naked, felt sense of being by itself—that subtle, kinesthetic sense of aliveness that we talked about—that is always present and utterly immune to any thoughts or opinions about the moment. It just is.

In this exercise, we will give it a go, using our reflection as an object of meditation, sensing into our deeper being while remaining compassionate and accepting of our unique self, with any attending comfortable and uncomfortable thoughts and feelings present in this moment. Mirror meditation is deep practice for being present but also a beneficial and powerful exercise in self-compassion and emotional resilience. Here, with our reflection, we practice loving acceptance. We allow ourselves to be as we are.

If we are suffering, this exercise invites us to see ourselves as people who need a little compassion and kindness. Mirror meditation encourages us to get beyond being the object of our criticism (marked by voices telling us things like, "I am a failure," "I am inadequate," and "I can't get it right").

The practice:

- Schedule a date with yourself. Intentionally pick an undistracted time and well-lit place to practice.
- Face yourself in the mirror in a comfortable position. Offer a Heart Salutation to yourself and the intention to be kind to yourself. Set a timer for five to ten minutes.
- Close your eyes and take a moment to notice your natural breath.
- Is it fast? Slow? Deep? Shallow? Then intentionally draw your breath in through your nose, relaxing as you exhale. Breathe evenly, but allow your out-breath to extend longer than your in-breath.
- Take a moment to go inward.
- Notice if your mind is distracted with thoughts about the day, such as your to-do list. Gently bring your attention away from those thoughts to your breath for a few moments. Inhale through the nose and let the exhale feel like golden light cascading down and through your body, releasing tension in different body parts. Do this a couple of times. You might wiggle your shoulders and neck, encouraging the body to relax anywhere that feels tense.
- Take a moment to notice what you are feeling.
- Tune in to your heart and chest area. Do you feel relaxed? Happy? Nervous? If you feel uncomfortable, can you allow yourself to be okay with that?
- Now open your eyes and look at yourself in the mirror.
- Gaze into your eyes. Pick one eye (left or right) and hold the gaze.

- Engage in a gentle, curious investigation of yourself in the mirror. Notice some of the following things:
- Does your breathing change when you look at yourself? If so, come back to an intentional steady breath.
- What is the tone of your gaze? Is it harsh or soft? If it feels intimidating, can you soften your gaze? Use your breath to help you. Steady breath, soft gaze.
- If you are feeling critical of yourself, look at your eyes. Do they look cold to you? If your eyes look cold or critical, take a moment to imagine yourself as the person who is receiving that kind of scrutiny. We tend to believe that we need to criticize ourselves to improve. But pay attention.
- Notice. How does it feel to receive that kind of critique? Does it feel helpful?
- Stay open to whatever arises.
- Notice sensations, thoughts, and emotions as they arise, and allow them to be there without needing to fix them.
- If your focus is becoming more critical and narrower, expand your peripheral vision to include your whole body. Relax. Watch the expansion and contraction.
- Notice the changes on your face as they occur.
- What happens when you feel challenging emotions?
- What happens when you relax, return to your breath, and soften your gaze?
- When the timer goes off, offer yourself a final Heart Salutation and thank yourself for the courage to face yourself in the mirror without judgment.

Notes: _____

_____

_____

_____

_____

_____

_____

_____

_____

Chapter 10

Getting Naked

Take off your clothes. Show me. Show me your edges.
I want to see with my own eyes where you end and where I begin.
I want to see where I fit, where you leave off being you and turn
into me.
—Unknown

So, now we're getting right down to it. Thus far, we've practiced relaxing and getting to know ourselves. We've befriended our thinking mind (without taking it seriously), learned to let thoughts dissipate, let go of trying to "know" everything, let guidance in, stretched our limits, healed our relationships, learned communication tips, and rested in simple Presence.

We're ready to unveil ourselves to the world—to drop our pretenses, thoughts, tensions, pressures, and desires. We're ready to *get naked* and share ourselves. Of course, we can always learn more about ourselves, but part of the process includes sharing ourselves with and being ourselves in the world.

Nowhere is this riskier than in our intimate relationships.

Dare I show myself as I am, warts and all? Can I open to allow another person to show their imperfect selves to me without judgment?

Renowned psychologist John Welwood wrote an article for *Science and Nonduality* magazine, whose title alone touches upon the power inherent in our relationships to wake us up—or what I call getting naked in the now. His article is called "Intimate Relationships as a Spiritual Crucible." In it, he examines the charnel ground of relationships where we acknowledge and work with our wounds, fears, and illusions. It sounds a bit daunting, posed this way, but it needn't be. We are entering the juiciest territory. It is freeing to bust through conditioning, show ourselves as we are, and embrace each other as a unique expression of human life. It engenders trust to share our deepest secrets with another.

Famed relationship guru and author of *Mating in Captivity: How to Keep Desire and Passion Alive in Long-term Relationships*, Esther Perel, says it this way: "This is the challenge of sexual intimacy, of bringing home the erotic. It is the most fearsome of all intimacies because it is all-encompassing. It reaches the deepest places inside us, and involves disclosing aspects of ourselves that are invariably bound up with shame and guilt. It is scary, a whole new kind of nakedness, far more revealing than the sight of our nude bodies."

Practicing with another helps us find the corners where we are not willing to look, for often, our partner is a mirror of our soul. We can approach this as we might an inviting lake and either dip a toe in tentatively at first or dive in with the attitude of joyful abandon. Whatever suits us. It doesn't matter so long as we get naked and wet and do so with a dollop of joyful anticipation.

Regardless, we must drop our self-centered agendas so that we may look and see the naked, sacred other—a reflection of ourselves—just as they are. And, to expose our deepest, darkest secrets, we must feel safe.

This journey we are on is a journey of love. It is a love we frequently seek in another before we realize that there is no other—only naked awareness—Now—that is love unfolding moment-to-moment.

Come with me as we arouse our natural curiosity, reclaim our aliveness, and dare to bare our souls to ourselves and another. This chapter is for lovers of all ages and inclinations. But don't worry; I will share some tips for exploring vulnerability with your partner to help you initiate transformational intimacy as we dive further into the juicy Now.

In this chapter we will be intentional about exploring vulnerability with our partner. We will create a safe space, ask deep questions, share uncomfortable secrets, practice communicating explicitly about sex and intimacy, and take a look at our conditioning that may be keeping us from feeling intimate and alive in the bedroom.

Let's practice!

Practice #25: Sacred Space

The Sacred Space is where you give yourself and your partner the opportunity to be transparent—to acknowledge who you are, what you feel, how you think, and, perhaps most important, how you can become more deeply available to each other.
—Margot Anand

My husband and I took a yearlong training during our most challenging time together. The extended workshop was called Love and Ecstasy Training by Margot Anand. It was a program designed to teach the participants how to discover and communicate how they liked to be loved. In it, we learned how to be vulnerable with another—to open to discussions that made us feel naked and exposed but also connected and intimate once shared. We talked about our innermost selves—our fears, our shame—making these talks much more vulnerable than other kinds of "hard" conversations, such as "Whose job is it to take out the garbage?" or "I felt hurt when you criticized me in public the other day" or "I feel overwhelmed by my child-rearing obligations and your expectations as to how clean the house should be." Still, like hard conversations, such talks benefitted from a tip on how and when to have them.

In our yearlong love and ecstasy training, we were taught early on about the concept of creating a "sacred space." We were to bring a little ritual to our intention to create a setting that would help us feel safe exploring the deeply vulnerable territory.

Jay and I set about co-creating our sacred space. We appreciated that the simple ritual already signaled to us that something *different* was happening—that we would act with more intention and awareness than we might ordinarily do in our day. Following the instruction, we began creating our sacred space for the first time, approaching it as collaborative play that we did together.

We knotted together a string of silk scarves, the color of the rainbow, to create a giant circle and then placed that around our bed to create an intentional demarcation of our sacred space. Next, we put some decorative touches on the night table featuring objects from our travels to remind us of the playfulness and fun we had together. Then, we put photos of our kids and handmade drawings to stand for the importance of family. Next, we added a string of twinkle lights and spritzed some of our favorite essential jasmine oil to evoke a sensual attitude. Finally, we smudged the space and each other with sage to symbolize clearing out any bad energy and starting fresh.

It may seem like a cumbersome idea to create a sacred space. But when you are intentionally voyaging into vulnerable territory—i.e., getting naked both inside and out, which might include sharing shameful secrets or preparing to face some deeply held piece of fear bravely—this simple gesture is significant. It signals that something different is happening, that space and time are being set aside for focused, fresh interaction.

Our brains need this little transition time and cues to help us change gears. For example, it can be tricky to go from taking out the garbage while juggling a toddler's or teen's needs to deep intimacy with another person. Contrary to popular belief, we can't do two or more things simultaneously; instead, we just quickly flick our attention from one thing to another. This splitting of our focus is exhausting and does not offer us the rest and attention that one-pointedness gives us.

For years, Jay and I used this trick of establishing a date time (don't overlook the lunch hour!) and then refreshing our sacred space. These few minutes signaled to each of us that, for the next hour or so, we would not be an engineer solving a problem, a program manager working on deadlines, or a parent carpooling kids. Instead, we were going to devote all our attention to one another. How did we know? We had taken a moment of transition time to set the stage intentionally. We'd turned off our phones and left them in another room, noted the sweet scent of jasmine in the air and the string of twinkle lights sparkling. Then, in anticipation, we'd step over the silk scarf threshold into our magic space where anything was possible. As we metaphorically left our everyday roles and expectations behind, we were available to be utterly attentive.

We had signaled through this routine that something new, fresh, and exciting was going to take place. We let go of the mundane, ordinary way of relating and set the stage for closeness, honesty, and respect. In the safety of our silk scarf circle, we became genuinely naked in the now with each other. We visited childhood hurts and fears, shared sexual fantasies, and dared to explore each other's bodies and minds in new ways. This magic circle was the sacred space we needed to create to feel safe and trust one another, attentive as we each explored being vulnerable and learning how to communicate what scared but secretly thrilled us, despite being resistant, fearful, and wounded. In this space, it was okay to explore. We didn't have to know anything, and it was okay to get uncomfortable sometimes.

Twenty-five years later, we still carry the vestiges of this practice. Our Sprinter van even bears a string of twinkle lights across the back of the bed that we can turn on to change the effect. Meanwhile, at home, we demarcated our entire bedroom as a sacred space for us — so we don't work in our bedroom, and we don't keep our phones plugged in at night in our bedroom.

Instead, we painted the walls a deep red and hung colorful silk saris on our bedframe to remind us of the fun of being playfully passionate. As a result, our bedroom is a sacred space;

the to-do lists get left behind, along with our analytical, judging roles that are important for work but not intimacy.

The practice:

- Talk with your partner about the idea of creating a sacred space to assist in going deeper with one another. Explain that a little ritual together can help us transition from everyday life to a setting that allows us to feel safe to explore intense or vulnerable territory.
- Have each of you gather a few meaningful objects to place on your sacred space altar. Think about things that symbolize being playful and loving together. Consider objects of beauty that capture the awe-inspiring for you or your partner. Add some decorative touches that effectively change the space: a candle, twinkle lights, a spritz of essential oil, or something such as our ring of silk scarves that stands as a threshold you will intentionally cross over. You might have some favorite massage lotion or oil available. Other ideas include designating a singular piece of cloth that you sit on, lie on, or drape nearby. Suppose you only use this piece of fabric for these intentional meetings. In that case, it will begin to have special meaning for you, symbolizing a mutual heartfelt desire to connect deeply, to open to vulnerability with your beloved.
- You can make this sacred space as simple or elaborate as feels right. Even lighting a single candle or piece of incense can signal a change from everyday life.
- Set a time for the engagement. (This also helps us transition from one way of being to another.)
- Clean yourselves: brush your teeth, and wash as necessary.

- As you gather in the space, take a moment to acknowledge each other. This acknowledgment might look like a deep, relaxing hug.
- With hands in prayer position, bow before the other. This gesture is called a Heart Salutation and symbolizes honoring the other as an aspect of yourself with the same divine spirit.
- Allow yourself to feel the titillation—electricity of excitement—present in the air as you ready to bare yourself before another. What you are doing together is scary and committing but deeply satisfying and enjoyable—like being at the apex of a roller coaster ride.
- Always close with a Heart Salutation before leaving the sacred space. (For twenty-five years, my husband and I have closed each session with eyes open, looking at one another, Heart Salutation, and the words: "I honor you as myself." It is one of the cornerstone demonstrations of our commitment to this journey together.)

Notes: _____

_____

_____

_____

_____

_____

_____

_____

Next, we'll talk about some activities you can do in your sacred space, but feel free to come up with your own ideas. Also, if you are doing self-inquiry work on your own—perhaps diving into past traumatic memories, it can be beneficial to set up a sacred

Getting Naked

space for yourself. This space might be an altar where you light a candle, or it could be a piece of clothing—anything to signal to yourself that you are leaving the mundane and entering into sacred time and space, holding yourself in a loving embrace.

Exploring vulnerability—asking deep questions and sharing uncomfortable secrets

To explore vulnerability and strengthen intimacy, we need to practice being transparent with ourselves and one another. I like to think of this as asking deep questions and sharing uncomfortable secrets—setting a foundation for meaningful conversations.

Being transparent (even to ourselves) requires us to shift from mundane living where we are focused on transactional questions about our day-to-day lives such as, "Did you pick up the dry cleaning?" "How was work?" "What do you want to eat for dinner tonight?", to exploring what moves our soul, inspires us, or motivates us along with sharing what holds us back, what we fear, and what we are ashamed of.

Oddly, in these juicy practices for getting present, we may need to travel back or forward in time, examining peak moments from our lives that left an indelible good or bad impression, or imagining living in accordance with our highest aspiration.

The next two practices are short prompts to get you started.

Practice #26: What Is Your Heart's Desire?

I remember hearing this question for the first time; it stopped me in my tracks. Nobody had ever asked me what my heart's desire was. The most similar was "What do you want to do with your life?" Typically, that morphed into questions like, "What do I want to study?" Or "What career do I want?" Maybe "What sports do I want to pursue?" So, I tended to look outward for answers.

I would think hard about my interests and natural proclivities. I love writing and collaborating, for instance. I'm good at spreadsheets and enjoy researching and finding things. I like teaching and managing complex programs. I love traveling and being outside. I would think about how to contribute positively to things that mattered to me, like global communication and conflict resolution. I'd also consider what was important to me, such as spending time with my kids and family. Then, I'd wonder, "Can I be a successful businesswoman and spend time with my kids?" "Should I homeschool?" Later, I'd mentally try to cross-reference all these desires to find an answer that honored them all.

But this question, "What is my heart's desire?" hit me differently. It dropped me down from my thinking head and into my heart. Immediately I felt that it was not a question to "think" about—at least not in the typical pros versus cons way of thinking. Instead, it felt like a question being asked of a different "me"—not the one that lived and worked in the world, but a different ineffable quality of "me-ness." My heart didn't know how to reason or come up with an answer, so initially, I could only answer, "I don't know." But the question lodged in my heart, and I began to open it inside. I began to notice what made me feel vibrantly alive inside. I realized that my heart's desire pointed to an attitude of living more than something discrete to do. I yearned to feel light-hearted and playful but also kind and compassionate. I wanted to embody unconditional love. Mainly, this question permitted me to stop figuring life out and gently ponder who I was and how my soul wanted to move, regardless of what I was *doing*.

Some questions rock our world and that of our loved ones. This question rocked mine. It is a question with the potential to root out our highest (think "spiritual") aspiration—not the one we think we *should* aspire to. It is a compelling practice to do by yourself, but also to do with another.

In the example above, I describe my solitary process after I heard this question. But my husband and I, in the sanctity of our sacred space, have also asked it of each other. We still revisit it from time to time.

It is one thing to gently ponder your heart's desire and another to share with your beloved what's happening inside as you search for resonance in answering the question. Because the question tends to take us out of worldly living and practical solutions, it can open the way to profound conversations. Once we know what someone's heart desires, we have deep insight into what makes them tick. When we ask another person this question and listen attentively to what comes up, we offer to help take care of their soul. That is the level of trust on the table.

The practice:
This is a simple, short practice. It does not need to be a formal and agreed-upon mission to ask this question.

Timing, however, is essential.

- Pick a time when you are relaxed, naturally quiet, and at ease with each other in sacred space—before or after lovemaking, before going to sleep, or in the early morning while you are still resting. It could even be when you are driving in the car (though probably not during a hectic morning commute). If relevant, you might refresh your sacred space by lighting a candle, putting on soft music, or resting together in a gentle embrace.

- Allow some silence to fill the space. Don't ask questions or make comments about daily life. Instead, allow your mind to drift away from the mundane. Rest, quietly present together.
- Allow yourself to be curious about your partner. Allow the possibility of learning something new — something different than their personality traits, unconnected to their skills or intellect.
- When you feel ready to listen attentively without comment, ask your partner, "What is your heart's desire?"
- Allow silence and space to be present while your partner ingests the question. Be mindful not to rush to fill the quiet by commenting on what they say or prodding them to answer. Instead, allow your full attention to be listening and attentive, even if there is only silence in reply.
- Be available to visit the question at another time.
- Don't forget to ask yourself too!

Notes: _____

_____

_____

_____

_____

_____

_____

_____

_____

"What is your heart's desire?" is one of my favorite questions because it takes me away from my ordinary way of thinking and perceiving the world. But feel free to try others!

Many questions can take us out of everyday life and spur interesting, meaningful conversations or inward contemplation. These might be questions about the past, such as, "What is your most cherished childhood memory?" or "What is your favorite characteristic about yourself?" or "What is something you want to try but are too scared to try?" If you are doing this with your partner, you might ask, "How do you like to be shown love?" or "What do you like best about our relationship?" If you are more focused on your journey, you can ask yourself, "What makes me feel passionately alive?" "What gives me courage?" Or "What are my core values?" (Though you can also ask those of your partner!)

If you want further inspiration, research "questions to build intimacy" or "questions for self-inquiry."

Practice #27: Tell Me a Secret

We've talked about asking yourself and others penetrating questions as the first part of the formula for becoming more transparent. The second part is to share painful secrets. (Note: these might even be things we can barely admit to ourselves!)

We may be entering tricky territory here. Some people find the best path forward is forgetting or ignoring challenging life experiences. So, for instance, my grandmother, who worked for the underground in Holland during WWII, may have had to do unspeakable things to survive, but she did survive. However, she refused to talk about or revisit that time for the rest of her life. Her attitude was, it's over and done. I'm moving on.

People also have differing opinions on whether privacy or transparency is critical in a relationship. We deem privacy essential but instinctively understand that keeping secrets can undermine trust while transparency engenders trust.

We must look to our motivation. Indeed, we are accountable for our happiness and must process life on our own privately. But privacy is different from keeping secrets.

Bruce Muzik, a relationship repair expert, helps us discern the difference between being private and keeping secrets in a relationship. He says a secret has three components: 1) intentionally hiding information, 2) feeling ashamed or afraid, and 3) knowing our partner would be upset at our hiding. The bottom line, secrets create walls to intimacy and much more.

Muzik also has a popular TEDx Talk called "The Big Secret Nobody Wants to Tell." In it, he says, "The secrets we hide have a devastating impact on our life. When we hide secrets, we are forced to lie about who we are... When we do that for long enough, we lose touch with who we authentically are, and the aliveness we once felt as children gets replaced by numbness."

Here, on this journey together, we seek to be in direct touch with that aliveness that comes from being who we authentically are. We want to experience the naked now — stripped of secrets. Then, hopefully, we get to share it too.

I don't know if my grandmother died feeling numb from keeping secrets. Concerning finding peace within myself, however, revisiting and exploring experiences marked with shame and fear have offered me the opportunity to heal — to redefine myself. For example, when scary flashbacks about childhood sexual abuse came up, one of the hidden, secret messages I took away was "I am a bad, dirty girl." *Is that so?*

Diving into those memories (the subject of my memoir *More… Journey to Mystical Union through the Sacred and the Profane*) was scary, triggered PTSD, and left me feeling spent. But I persisted and even shared these memories with my husband. Eventually, I sensed that I had done the best a small child could at the time and did not have to carry the stigma of shame with me any longer. Then came a juicy grown-up's perspective: I am happily married in a committed relationship; what's wrong with being a "dirty girl" now?

Transparency not only offered me a path to peace, but it has offered my husband and me a path back to intimacy. It takes trust to bare one's soul. During our darkest times, we turned the corner and began a practice of transparency.

Over the years, we developed a code sentence, "Tell me a secret," that invites us to explore our shameful, hidden shadows together. "Tell me a secret" has led us to expose unbearable, regrettable acts we wish we'd never done, admit beliefs we harbor about ourselves, and reveal hidden fantasies. We practice active listening as the door to our partner's secrets, feeling the honor of being a vessel of trust into which they can pour their secrets.

I still vividly remember my husband telling me the whole truth about his affair. We were on our way out to dinner alone, and it was raining. I asked him a question, possibly about the affair, and he pulled the car over and stopped on the side of the road.

He turned to me and said, "I have to tell you something."

My heart flip-flopped as I waited. The air was electric.

"It was more than a one-night stand," he said. "It started a couple of months ago…"

And then he proceeded to tell me the whole story.

Sitting there in the car on that rainy night, listening to him tell me things I didn't want to hear, offering to answer any questions, had a strange effect on me. I felt closer to him than I could have imagined in those sharing moments. I saw his courage. I felt honored that he would tell me the truth, however painful it was. It was an opening back to intimacy.

Now, when one or the other of us utters those words, "Tell me a secret," a tiny trill of excitement runs through me. We have no real secrets between us anymore, but the words have come to mean *I want to feel close to you* combined with the juicy understanding that I am lovable exactly as I am, warts and all.

This next practice is very similar to the previous one, but instead of looking forward to how we want to be, we look backward at moments that have shaped our lives.

The practice:
This is another simple, short practice. Like asking the question, "What is your heart's desire?" timing is essential.

Working with this question takes a lot of courage and the willingness to reciprocate. You might want to talk about the concept a little. You can say that you read how taking turns sharing difficult things and practicing listening attentively but without comment can strengthen intimacy.

- Pick a time when you are relaxed, naturally quiet, and at ease with each other. You may already be in a sacred space, perhaps before or after physical intimacy, wherever and whenever you feel safe. Imagine what times are best for your partner to be open and available. Pick a moment when neither of you is too tired or facing a deadline. Bedtime can seem like a good time, but one or the other partner is often too tired after a busy day.

- As in the previous exercise, allow some silence to fill the space and to transition away from daily life. Rest, quietly present together.

- Think of things in your own life that you feel ashamed or shy to talk about—maybe things nobody else knows. These might include secret fantasies or regrettable acts.

- Then, there are two ways of going from here: You can initiate the intimacy by saying, "Can I tell you a secret?" or you can encourage your partner to go first by asking, "Will you tell me a secret?" (with the understanding that you will reciprocate).

- Allow a feeling of trepidation or uncomfortableness to be present. This kind of bold sharing takes tremendous courage, where we risk opening authentically, not knowing how our partner will respond. So, it's natural to feel trepidation. But know this, you can feel scared sharing or nervous listening and do it anyway.

- If your partner goes first in sharing, listen carefully. Your initial response might be nothing more than "Thank you for sharing," followed by silence. It takes tremendous courage to share that which we have secreted away. We are honoring the bravery.

- If you go first, make sure your partner is open to listening at that time. You can admit how scared you might feel to share, and you can also tell your partner you don't need them to respond; you want to practice sharing hard things. Finally, after sharing, remember to thank your partner for listening.

- The hard part might be that your partner does not respond exactly how you hoped. Maybe your partner gets triggered and feels scared or angry. That's okay. It can be part of the practice not only to practice sharing difficult things but giving your partner a moment to feel whatever they felt in response. Thank your partner anyway. We are learning how to communicate hard things and how to listen when hard things are shared. We are *practicing*; we don't have to be perfect.

- Later, you can revisit the idea of sharing and listening without comment. We skinny-dip in and learn together how to support one another in sharing scary things.

Notes: _____

_____

_____

_____

_____

_____

_____

_____

Communicating about pleasure

Asking profound questions like "What is your heart's desire?" and sharing uncomfortable, shameful memories when prompted to "Tell me a secret" opened us to the idea of communicating more than only grunts and exclamations during sex.

Intimacy, we realized, could be cultivated and nurtured. Intimacy was more than just a passionate physical encounter—

it required us to bare our souls right alongside our bodies. So, while we peeled back the boundaries to intimacy by sharing things that had nothing to do with either sex or the practical details of managing a busy life together, we also practiced focusing on the nitty-gritty details we experienced during lovemaking.

In bed, in some ways, we had to throw out all our assumptions about sex—and learn how to experiment together, try new things, and talk about what felt good and what didn't feel good. Not having to know beforehand took away a huge burden. We could learn!

Communication played a considerable role in our yearlong training. First, we broke down practices and focused on small steps. Then, after every piece, we learned to offer feedback, talking about what the experience had been like for us—what we liked and didn't like. As a result, we lost our fear of being too clinical in bed or not instinctively knowing what our partner or we wanted and instead developed the habit of being willing to try new things and talk about them. Willingness and communication catapulted our sex life into hot new territory.

Over the years, and with the right audience, it's something I love to share.

Practice #28: That Feels Good

In 1997, my husband and I and our two little kids found ourselves in Yelapa, Mexico—a town on the edge of the ocean, accessible only by boat, thrust up against the mountainous jungle. The outer setting felt exposed and vulnerable to the elements. The house we lived in, a "palapa," didn't even have enclosed walls to insulate us, only half walls. The setting amid coconut trees and lush foliage with white sandy beaches and flocks of birds dancing on the breeze, however, made it seem like paradise; but we knew deadly scorpions were lurking. We carefully lifted each cushion to check for them.

We were here by choice, and we were excited instead of afraid of being exposed and vulnerable, as it reflected our inner journey for the last year, post affair. We had spent the prior twelve months studying SkyDancing under Margo Anand. Margot opened our hearts and minds to the idea of going into our scared, hurt places and sharing our experiences. We appreciated our work to eradicate the scorpions from our minds and rekindle the intimacy. Talk about transparency!

Amidst the din and contrast that made up Yelapa—a New Age gringo enclave superimposed on a Mexican fishing village—we had met people from around the world. One couple practiced Ayurvedic medicine and offered unique Shirodhara treatments, dripping warm oil on the forehead to soothe and invigorate the senses. A woman had studied Sufi dancing and facilitated a Sufi-dancing circle. Another had come with her four kids and brought loads of board games we'd play together. Another shared yoga practice.

We also wanted to share something precious and came up with the idea of offering a mini Tantra workshop. We put together a program focused on the importance of communication in cultivating intimacy.

In that sweet little casita perched on the edge of the cliff, we did an exercise where one partner massaged only the face of the other. With each subtle and gentle movement, the one receiving would tune in and describe how it felt. The giver would vary the touch in tempo, location, strength, and rhythm, and the receiver would then report whether they liked it or not. This facial massage focuses on tiny sensations and teaches us to pay attention to how it feels, what we want, and how to communicate that to our partner. It's incredible how much sensation resides on the face alone.

When I learned the importance of sharing in detail what I sensually liked and didn't like, I was astounded. Somehow, I had never thought of communicating about physical intimacy explicitly. I had never thought about practicing together to bring one another more pleasure and satisfaction or to stretch my limits about what I thought I liked. I had not even wondered if I knew what I wanted or didn't like. Nor had I thought about taking turns and then talking about it. For me, lovemaking was a quiet, concurrent, instinctual activity.

For the first ten years of our marriage, I was a silent sex partner, barely uttering a sound. I harbored a deep shame about sex that I wasn't even aware of. I thought feeling pleasure and having an orgasm were private things. In a way, it felt like a secret. My husband said he never knew when I had an orgasm because I tried to hide it. But as I began using my words to talk about my secrets, I also found my voice in bed.

What was happening was we were busting through our ideas and beliefs about intimacy. The hidden conditioning in society is that we are supposed to know what we like and don't like and anticipate what our lover will or won't like. In our training, we learned a different protocol: 1) Take turns focusing on your pleasure and 2) discover and share what you like and don't like. The old me might have thought it sounded too clinical, but the new me appreciated this fresh way of thinking. Who knew you could get better at sex and intimacy?

This next practice is a place to start, based on that facial massage workshop we taught twenty-five years ago in Yelapa.

The practice:

- Agree on a time and place where you will practice facial massage.
- Bring a little reverence to the moment by refreshing your sacred space beforehand. (Remember, this ritual can be as simple as lighting a candle or incense or playing soft music.)
- Decide who will go first and how long each massage will be.
- The receiver closes their eyes and allows the giver to touch their face and neck, including the head and ears. The idea is for the giver to move deliberately from one area of the head to another and to vary the touch, trying light touch and firm touch, quick or slow movements, as well as different rhythms.
- The giver allows pauses between massage segments to enable the receiver to process and reflect on how it feels to them.

- **Ideas of ways to massage the head, face, and neck**
  - Rub under the apple of the cheeks, down toward the jawline.
  - Sweep softly under the eyes moving outward.
  - Make a circular motion around the eye, moving up and around.
  - Rub the ears.
  - Scratch the top of the head, lightly or hard.

- ◦ Massage the back of the neck in varying degrees of firmness.
- ◦ Hold the points at the bottom back of the skull firmly, massaging in little circles.
- ◦ Massage the temple area.
- ◦ Sweep the hands over the entire face.
- ◦ Hold palms over both the eyes.
- ◦ Massage the upper lip.
- ◦ Massage the outer cheekbones near the ears.
- ◦ Try blowing on different areas of the face.
- ◦ Try tapping or fluttering the fingers.
- ◦ Bring two fingers from each hand to the center of the forehead and ever so lightly wipe away toward the outside.

- The receiver is to communicate how the different touches feel to them. We are learning how to discern what we like and don't like and how to get comfortable speaking about it. As the massage continues, we have more information, so we can begin comparing different sensations.
- The receiver may say simple things like "That feels good" as it is happening, but also things like, "When you massaged my cheeks firmly, my whole face relaxed," or "I love it when you rub my ears," "I never noticed how much I love my forehead being lightly stroked," or "I like the firm touch best."
- It might sound cumbersome to practice communicating this way, but it is worth it. First, we must become familiar with ourselves on our journey to being psychologically naked in the now. Then in the continued journey to physical intimacy with another, we must get comfortable sharing and communicating how we feel.

Notes: _____

_____

_____

_____

_____

_____

_____

_____

_____

Overcoming conditioning and expectations

An exercise like the one above can expose our conditioning about receiving or giving pleasure. What ideas do you have about yourself or someone else feeling pleasure? Is pleasure something to be felt but not talked about?

It also might open the door to see other conditioning and expectations about love, sex, and intimacy that we may have unwittingly adopted. So often, we block ourselves from exploring further intimacy because we have a deep-seated belief about how things should be or how we should be.

If we want to live naked in the now—in tune with our authentic being—in addition to learning how to communicate, we must learn to investigate our conditioned beliefs and ideas. Like many other exercises in this book, this begins by asking questions. Sex is a ripe and challenging area to dive into but worth our time.

What are the "shoulds" we harbor about sex? Do they still serve us? Is there a shameful component to sex that we adopted when we were young that we can revisit now as adults? (Recall my story about feeling ashamed that I was a "dirty girl" for being the object of childhood sexual abuse, then reclaiming the right to be a "dirty girl" as a married adult.)

This next practice invites us to slow down and take a moment to listen to our beliefs about sex, love, and intimacy. Of course, it's natural to have developed ideas about sex based on our upbringing and the life circumstances we have lived. Our goal here is to investigate whether our beliefs are still serving our highest good or whether they are blocking us and causing us suffering.

Practice #29 Am I Naughty or Nice? Can I Be Both?

During a quiet, contemplative moment, perhaps before bed or while taking a tea break, intentionally tune into your beliefs about sex, love, and intimacy—especially those you formed during childhood or what you have picked up through societal conditioning about how to look or act during sex.

The practice:
One of the easiest ways is by asking yourself questions. Below are some to get started:

- Do you have beliefs about:
  - what a "good girl or boy" would or would not do?
  - what "sexy" looks like?
  - what acceptable bedroom behavior is?
  - who you should be attracted to?
  - what you like and don't like?
  - Have you concluded that you are "too old," "too fat," "too skinny," or "too something else" to be attractive?
  - Do you believe your partner should anticipate your needs?
  - Have you decided something is not for you without even trying it?
  - Do you think intimacy is instinctual rather than learned?
  - How do you feel about talking about sex with your partner?

- Another way to peek inside is to do a freewriting experiment (like *Write Now Mind*).
  - Set a timer for five minutes.
  - Remember the rules:

- ◦ Keep Your Hand Moving
- ◦ Be Specific
- ◦ Lose Control
- ◦ Don't Think

- • Write to each of the following prompts:
  - ◦ Sex should be...
  - ◦ Intimacy is...
  - ◦ I like/don't like sex because...
  - ◦ I want my partner to...
  - ◦ I feel ashamed of...
  - ◦ Being sexy is...
  - ◦ In bed, I'm afraid to...

Notes: _____

_____

_____

_____

_____

_____

_____

_____

At the very start of this book, I suggested we would embark on this journey with the curious eye of a child and the investigative nature of a detective or scientist. All we need is a little willingness to begin questioning our beliefs and to take our inquiry with a playful light heart. One of the easiest and most fun ways to keep investigating is to invite in the spirit of play.

This next chapter has some playful ideas to get you started. Some are games you can play with friends, others with lovers.

Chapter 11

For Play

We are never more fully alive, more completely ourselves, or more deeply engrossed in anything than when we are playing.
— Charles E. Schaefer

Humor and play are possibility, possibility invites change, change invites healing.
— Esther Perel, *Mating in Captivity*

This chapter is for friends *and* lovers. We will explore new ways to play together as adults, including a sensory awakening ritual, partner kriyas (a type of yoga) designed to strengthen and improve relationships, and a daring sexy "date night" game for intimate partners to enliven or re-enliven their relationship. In each of these, we will dive deep into the sensual art of now, traveling beyond what we think we know to remember the art and joy of playing.

Thus far, we have explored all kinds of practice tools that help us experience the present moment, so this is not any different, but it's something we can do with others. The process is delightful when we are intimate with the moment *and* sharing that with another. You need to look no further than this chapter's titillating enticements to play with another for the juiciest path to the naked now.

But before we embark on our juicy play interlude, let's ask the question: What is play?

Stuart Brown, the National Institute for Play founder, says that play offers a sense of engagement and pleasure by taking the player out of a sense of time and place, such that "the experience of doing it is more important than the outcome."

Playing helps us focus on what is immediately before us, enlivening our experience and intimately connecting us to the moment. We are immersed in our senses, filled with the scent of grass, the touch of sandstone, the taste of sweet water quenching our thirst, the feel of sweat dripping, and the sound of an eagle's cry caught on the breeze. We are in touch with what I call the "sensual art of now."

I can hear our minds spinning, searching for meaning. *The sensual art of now?*

"Relax. Close your eyes. Bring all your attention to your body. Feel the chair beneath your seat. Feel the ground beneath your feet. Notice the slight breeze traveling through your nostrils as you breathe."

These are the words a spiritual teacher might say to guide participants into meditation. Gently, these words bring our attention back to the present. Back to now—away from the persistent analyzing, judging, interpreting, comparing, trying to improve, and searching for meaning in the voices of our egoic mind—voices that keep our attention rooted somewhere other than right here, right now.

That's also what happens when we play.

The mind, especially the adult mind, is habituated to *think* about life rather than experience it nakedly. That's okay. That is the mind's job. But we are more than just our minds. And, I assure you, we are all secretly yearning to nakedly experience it—to enter into a moment so fully immersed that we forget our worries. I call this proceeding without knowing or expecting. It used to happen when we were innocently at play, innovating as we went. Something got lost along the way. Now, with all the seriousness of adult life, what we deeply yearn for is to play.

So, how do we regain that joyful innocence?

We cultivate an attitude of play, an openness of mind, and an air of the unexpected. We get rooted in the sensual now.

Let's take off our adult robes. The following practices are just for *play*!

Practice #30: Sensory Awakening Ritual

I love to talk about the sensual art of now because it calls to mind one of my favorite playful sensory awakening rituals I learned many years ago at a SkyDancing Tantra retreat, led by Margot Anand. Of course, the word "sensual" makes it sound erotic, and it can be. But it is also a fun and refreshing game appropriate to various settings and players. I have recreated this ritual with my husband, Jay, as part of our date night, with groups of friends, writing colleagues, and on retreat with fifty people. Everyone loves it.

Maybe we have forgotten how to play in our busy, grown-up, responsible lives. No worries. We can re-learn how. Let's do it! Let's get back to the sensual art of now and engage with the moment in a spirit of light-hearted curiosity. Even better, let's do it together!

In this next sensory awakening ritual, we will create a magical moment, like a birthday, holiday, graduation, or other event when we shower one another with love, attention, good food, drinks, and presents. Then, we will travel to the realm of senses, one at a time, adding an element of titillation and mystery.

What grown-up doesn't love a little mystique to spice things up and put us in a playful mode?

In this ritual, one person will be the Giver, the other(s) the Receiver (s). Each Receiver will wear a blindfold while the Giver introduces them to a sensual experience, one at a time. A taste experienced fully without sight can be uniquely different and infinitely richer as our mind opens to the experience and notices subtleties; hence, the popularity of "wine tasting," for example. A smell fully experienced at this moment can inexplicably transport us to another time, a distant memory.

Instead of the world being a set of known facts, a more poetic and timeless interpretation is available.

There is great fun in both the giving and receiving. As blindfolded Receivers, we enter the moment without knowing or expecting what is coming. As Givers, we relish the opportunity to create a sensual feast for someone else.

The preparation

First, each Receiver will need a blindfold. The blindfold adds the air of mystique. Formal blindfolds are not necessary; any scarf that completely covers the eyes will do.

Then, as Giver, you will need to plan and gather samples representative of each of the senses. (You may need to decide ahead of time whether you will do one sample for each scent or multiple. When I do it with a group, I stick with one, but for date night, I might have several of each.)

On the appointed date day, the Giver should have each of these ready but hidden from view.

Sounds: Musical instruments such as bells, gongs, singing bowls, flutes, guitars, etc., are always good, but so too are song samples or unusual sounds from the ocean or space or nature.

Smells: Essential oils are always a good option, but you might also consider flowers, spices, or soaps—anything that has a potent scent. If you are doing more than one scent, think of the order. For example, you might want to do cleansing scents like peppermint or eucalyptus before sensual scents like jasmine or ylang ylang.

Taste: Sensuous foods such as seedless grapes, bread and honey, chocolate, pineapple, and liquids such as fruit juice or liqueurs.

Touch: Fabrics, such as silk or fur, brushes, peacock feathers, rocks, or crystals.

Sight: You might use a photo, a beautiful rock, or something resembling an inkblot. On date night you can use your body, face, and eyes.

Optional items to have handy

- A Gong for starting each session,
- Toothpicks, Q-tips, small cups—to help with passing out samples, and
- Paper and pens for each participant—for freewriting feedback after each sense.

The practice:

- Schedule an undistracted time and place.
- Gather everything you need, including the blindfold(s) and samples. These should be organized perhaps on trays but kept hidden. (Note: remember to make sure no recipients have allergies.)
- Depending on whether you are doing this as a date night game with only your lover or an ice breaker at a work event, you may have more or less fanfare going in.
- For date night, you could sequester the Receiver in another room while you get the other room ready. You could light candles, have special seating available, and maybe some mood music before starting. Then blindfold them and bring them ceremoniously into the room, weaving a tale about taking them on a journey to an ancient temple or something.
- For groups, it works just as well to create the experience of anticipation by simply asking all participants to put on their blindfolds. It can feel scary wearing a blindfold— like a loss of control, so their mere donning creates an

instant unique experience. With groups, it can be fun to have them take off their blindfold in between and free-write for two minutes about the encounter. Then, you can invite people to share, which is a beautiful way to create group intimacy throughout the experience.

- Once the blindfolds are on, consider starting each session by ringing a gong or singing bowl. You can even use a gong found on an app like Insight Timer. Invite the receivers to listen to the gong sound as it slowly fades into nothing. (Note: Some people play different music the whole time, but I prefer to separate the senses completely. So, between each of the sense experiences below, I ring the gong, waiting until no sound is left. The gong sound demarcates one sense experience from the next and gets the recipient[s] recentered again.)

- Start with your first sense. I usually start with hearing, but some people like to start with smelling.

- *Hearing*: Play the sound for about thirty seconds to one minute. Allow some silence after each sound. Tibetan bells, singing bowls, and gongs are always fun to play, but if you don't have any, recordings of these are also good. In some situations, allowing the sound to come from different directions can be fun by walking around the room. There are other ways to create an unusual experience with sound. You can play something mysterious or at different frequencies. Get creative! My favorite is a segment (without the commentary) from Jim Wilson's *God's Chorus of Crickets*.

- *Smelling*: Allow the receiver to inhale the scent deeply without touching it to their face. (Hint: if you are using essential oils, you can dip these in Q-tips and hand them to the receiver.) Allow some minutes to pass between scents. The pause creates a delicious feeling of anticipation. When

I do this with a group, I often use ylang ylang because almost nobody recognizes it.

- *Tasting*: Using toothpicks or cups, bring the food or drink near the Receiver's nose allowing them to smell it first before inviting them to open their mouth and receive it. The smell is a significant component of taste. For date night, you might tease your lover a bit, maybe running the grape around their lips but retracting before they bite down, or dipping your finger into a liqueur and rubbing it on their lips. Don't be afraid to try radically different tastes, but end on something you know will be pleasing, like chocolate. When I do this with a group, I only do one sample taste. Often, I do carrot juice because it is tough to identify. My favorite comment one participant shared before she knew what it was, is "This is what green tastes like!"

- *Touching*: You will likely do this radically different depending on if you are doing it in a group setting or for date night. For date night, you might start almost imperceptibly with a very light touch of a feather or soft fur. Then, allow yourself to cover all different parts of the body teasingly, seductively, even maddeningly. In a group setting, I go for the unexpected and often hand out thundereggs which feel like hard clots of dirt on the outside, belying the beauty inside.

- *Seeing*: Again, how you handle this for date night versus friend or colleague night will likely be different. Either way, allow some silence to be in place before instructing the receivers to remove their blindfolds. On date night, it is remarkable to have your partner remove their blindfold and end with soul gazing and a melting hug. In a group setting, on the other hand, you may have an item sitting before each person—a photo, tarot card, or piece of nature. I often use a halved thunderegg for sight. Each thunderegg is unique and serves as an "inkblot" image. Then, during the freewriting feedback, people can write about what they see.

- Feedback is vital to help anchor the experience. On date night, it might just be a quiet sharing of what you liked or what took you by surprise. In a group setting, I love to invite each sense to end with a two-minute freewriting exercise.

- Finally, remember, if only two of you are there, you will eventually want to exchange roles. Save the exchange for a different day, though, so as not to water down the experience and to allow the new Giver ample time to prepare.

Notes: _____

_____

_____

_____

_____

_____

_____

_____

Partner Yoga

Doing exercises with a friend often makes the activity more fun and engaging. We love to go for walks with our friends, take aerobics classes together, and participate in sports with others. One of the things Jay and I learned along the way was partner yoga. Partner yoga means doing yoga poses with two people. Simple stretches with a partner can increase our range of motion and help us honor our commitment to stretch. Nowadays, you can find numerous partner yoga classes and forms such as partner vinyasa flow or AcroYoga.

Like many activities we do with one another, partner yoga can help us play and nourish each other. Elysabeth Williamson (internationally recognized as the foremost authority on partner yoga and the author of *The Pleasures and Principles of Partner Yoga*) cites these five benefits:

It connects and relaxes us.

It supports our yoga practice.

It creates more authenticity and honesty.

It allows us to see how we are in the relationship.

It deepens our capacity for intimacy.

I highly encourage you to try it!

Here, we will dive into one practice to get you started. It is one that we learned over twenty-five years ago and still practice regularly today. It is a practice that combines a simple pose and breathwork.

You can do it with your beloved partner or a close friend. Don't underestimate the potential of this one practice to enliven and deepen your relationship!

Practice #31: Venus Kriya

Kundalini yoga is an ancient Eastern practice made popular in the US through Yogi Bhajan. It combines the study of life-force energy and spiritual philosophy. *Yoga Journal* describes Kundalini yoga as a practice "that helps you channel powerful energy and transform your life." Today, even in the West, it has become a practice that is recognized to offer mental health benefits, comparing it with cognitive behavioral therapy and stress education.[ii]

In 1995, a mid-life crisis led Jay and me to investigate how to be happy within ourselves and as a couple. We began pursuing Eastern philosophy alongside Western therapy. We became curious about the concept of awakening "Kundalini." Kundalini is said to be an intrinsic life-force energy that lies coiled and dormant within us at the base of our spine until awakened. We had heard that you could experience expanded consciousness if you triggered it. We had also heard that practicing specific partner exercises helped combine your energies, and you might even experience shared consciousness. We weren't sure what it meant but were excited to investigate it ourselves. So, we signed up for a Kundalini yoga class for couples in Seattle. Later we also attended a White Tantra Yoga camp taught by disciples of Yogi Bhajan.

During that initial class, we learned a Venus Kriya (there are many). The one we practiced was an exercise that included soul gazing with your palms facing and touching each other while fire breathing together (a kind of short, fast, shallow, forceful breath).

While I can't speak to the science of what happens during a Venus Kriya, I will say it is one of the practices that has stuck with us for the last twenty-five years. One we do regularly. I find it to be an engaging, bonding activity, signaling that we are committed to the same path of exploring the unknown realm of consciousness together. At the end of a few minutes, the room stills, the air feels surreal, and my body tingles with aliveness. I feel calm and also profoundly in communion with Jay. It is a compelling way to connect and takes only three minutes.

The practice:

- Sit on the floor facing each other with knees touching in a rock pose (a kneeling position where your knees and legs are together, and you are resting on your heels) or, alternately, sit in chairs facing each other. (Jay and I sit on chairs.)
- You can set a timer for two or three minutes or allow the exercise to conclude naturally.
- Raise both hands cactus style to chest height, palms facing outward, and touch your partner's palms.
- Establish eye contact (i.e., begin Soul Gazing — see Practice #23). Remember to keep your gaze from shifting; look into only one of your partner's eyes.
- Allow a moment to pass while you feel the palms touching and receive each other's gaze.
- Take a deep breath together through your nostrils.
- Begin fire breathing (a series of short, forceful exhales through the nose while drawing in the abdomen) together for two to three minutes. (See Appendix A for more detailed instructions on how to fire breathe.)
- When one of you feels ready to stop fire breathing, signal the end by drawing in slowly, thoroughly, and deeply on the inhale. The other partner should match them.
- Allow the exhale to release slowly and naturally.
- Drop your hands to your lap.

- After a moment, close with hands in prayer and bow to the other.

Notes: _____

_____

_____

_____

_____

_____

_____

_____

Games lovers play

Years ago, a friend told me a story that stuck. It had to do with the quirky things we couples do that bring us closer together and the value of appreciating and identifying those things before it is too late. At the time, her marriage was on rocky ground. She and her husband were both busy professionals and had a young son, but it looked like they wouldn't make it. So, I asked her what she thought had happened.

She said, "Well, I think it is because we moved."

That made some sense to me. So, I mumbled about how stressful moving was, which could strain a marriage.

She said, "Oh no, it wasn't like that at all. The move was great. We weren't really stressed at all. We were excited to move to the new place, which was much bigger, nicer, and closer to work too."

"Oh, really? Well, what happened?"

"Well, I didn't think too much about it at the time because the new place is so nice looking but... it doesn't have a bathtub."

"A bathtub?"

"Yeah. Our old house only had this old bathtub—no shower. We used to curse it but had turned it into a fun thing—our thing. We'd put our son to bed every night, get naked, and bathe together. There were no distractions, and that time in the bathtub was when we would talk about life and connect. When we moved to the new place, we lost that. We each took our showers in the nice fancy bathroom and then went about our separate ways—reading or working in bed because that was also our habit. Somehow without those few precious moments in the bathtub, we stopped connecting. We stopped having undistracted time together. We lost touch with each other."

And there it was. The bathtub had been a sanctuary—a sacred place where they got naked and connected—a place to be undistracted from one another.

Since then, I've talked to many couples interested in what their "bathtub" is. Sometimes it is a ritual like this bathtub, where the partners get naked and physically touch each other, but it is something else altogether for others.

One couple I know bonded over farting. For most of us, farting is a borderline unacceptable activity in public—something one really "should not" do, and yet there is a moment in many relationships when we cross over that "unacceptable" boundary and risk farting in each other's presence—as if testing the waters. Will you love me when?

In the one couple's case, they had discovered they relished being able to fart in each other's presence. Instead of feeling ostracized or daring to let a little pop out, the couple laughed together. Farting became synonymous with being light-hearted and not taking life's "shoulds" too seriously. A fart became their secret code for choosing playfulness over seriousness. It was a type of foreplay—or, as I quip, "for play!"

We couples must remember to play with each other: to get naked and open, to let 'er rip—if that's our thing.

So, I ask you, what is your bathtub?

In other words, where in your relationship are you willing to unbutton the suit, get naked and present, and play with each other? When do you drop your "shoulds and shouldn'ts" or your ongoing to-do list and be natural with another?

We might hide it in a silly antic (like farting) or a simple ritual (like bathing together); maybe it is in a pat on the butt as we pass in the kitchen, or in a nickname of endearment we toss out. Pay attention. What about these things allows us to feel momentarily connected with another?

I posit that in these seemingly innocuous rituals we do with each other lies a superpower.

The power of play.

Play has the power to both unleash the present moment and allow us to share it with another.

"Play?" you ask. "I don't have time to play!" you might cry. "There's far too much work to be done—careers to manage, children to raise, soccer games to drive to, dishes to wash, beds to be made, not to mention endless problems to solve—the tub won't drain, the internet stopped working, I lost my keys."

I know, and I get it. Life is perpetually busy. We need to manage challenging schedules and meet deadlines. And there are "serious" things that require my attention: my child is getting bullied, my mother is losing her mind, my spouse is addicted to drugs, the world is going to hell in a racist hand-basket, and I can't talk to my old best friend because she believes the polar opposite of me.

But hear me out. We risk becoming hardened and dried up if we become entrenched in doing and trying to fix all the things we perceive are wrong. As a result, we can overlook the simple, juicy joy of "being" already present when we are light-hearted and playful with each other.

In the bathtub story, the couple perceived that they needed a better, bigger, fancier house closer to work in order to be happy. In reaching for greener grass, they overlooked that they would give up a playful ritual that made them feel connected and joyful. And the fancier house meant higher bills, which meant working more, hanging out less. They began taking life more seriously and eventually lost the ability to enjoy each other in the simplest way—naked in an old bathtub.

Of course, we can still get bigger houses closer to work, but as necessary: we need to play. The point is, we must occasionally thrill each other with our undistracted attention, free of agenda.

I am not saying to let go of being disciplined and organized. On the contrary, these help us structure our lives in positive ways. But suppose we want to touch into the joy of being naked in the now with another. In that case, we must be willing to let go of our plan and embrace a light-hearted whimsy—a coy look, a daring fart, a "come hither" attitude that beckons our partner into the unknown Now with us to play.

Frivolity and unstructured time together keep the creative, wild, messy spirit alive within us. That unpredictable spirit keeps us juicy, and juicy is good.

Let's face it; intimacy is messy. Physically it comes with all sorts of bodily juices escaping the confines of the body. Mentally and emotionally, it is the same. When we feel emotionally and spiritually intimate, we are not all buttoned up and acting per a plan; we are crying out in pleasure or pain, sharing the good, bad, and ugly of ourselves, wanting to be seen, loved, and accepted as we are. And we relish seeing this in another. We feel connected when someone is vulnerable with us.

I invited you a few pages ago to reflect on what your "bathtub" might be. I asked under what circumstances you unbutton your metaphorical suit and dare to be utterly au natural with another, no pretenses. Don't despair if nothing immediately pops into your mind; take a moment of reflection to ponder gently. Take the question with the same light-hearted attitude it invites you to find. Pay attention. Notice. When do you drop your guard with another? When does a momentary feeling of delight creep over you? I bet it's when you are feeling relaxed and a little playful.

After years of awareness practice, this is what I've discovered. When we are playful, we lose our persistent self-centered perspective, and in doing so, we meld with another.

Not sure what I mean?

Let's see if this helps. Often, we carry a self-image, a "sense of self" that feels like who we are. Our sense of self tends to have a measure of seriousness to it. We value being unique and special, of being able to pin down who we are. But not only is that constantly changing, there is an expense to that feeling. That identification with a defined sense of self encourages a feeling of separateness from the world. It inhibits our experience of union.

Here's the thing: that sense of self is not as solid as it seems. So, while it sounds scary to let our identification with it lapse, it already does that on its own. It comes and goes—like clothing that we put on. But the good news is that certain things naturally allow us to relax and take off our sense-of-self cloak, which contributes to our being effortlessly present instead of continually trying to keep up our self-image.

For instance, when we are silly and playing, we lose some of that rigid sense of self. We are less "discrete person" playing, and more playing itself. People often talk about this with things like dancing, saying there is a moment when you are no longer a person dancing but only the dancing itself.

Also, when we play, we can wriggle out of old roles and try on new ones—roles we don't typically adopt. We can pretend we are courageous or confident or perhaps shy and introverted. We can let go of our ideas and discover new things about ourselves and each other.

This loss of our sense of self that I am alluding to here does not have to be something momentous. Instead, it often happens in the simplest moments—ones we might overlook. I call these little moments of delight. So, for instance, when a butterfly alights on my hand, I might be momentarily overcome with joy. My eyes twinkle, my cheeks become apples, and I feel pure satisfaction. My particular personality is irrelevant to my feeling of delight.

This loss of sense of self can happen momentarily when we see a beautiful sunset or while listening to moving music. It might happen when we dangle a string in front of our cat and watch the antics. In such moments, nothing is more pressing than the delight itself. We are momentarily at one with the world.

Losing ourselves (in a good way) can also happen in our relations with others. So we can look for the moments when we naturally drop our cloak of selfness and are open to meld with another—our little playful rituals where we let down our invisible guard.

We can also cultivate such moments.

I suggest that we start to cultivate more of these by awakening an attitude of playfulness within us. So, slip that coy look on while making dinner and set a date to spend some frivolous time together.

This attitude begins a red-hot journey to holy intimacy. The following practice is sure to shake things up!

Practice #32: The Yin Yang Game

Let's face it. We men and women who openly read *Eat, Pray, Love* and stealthily (perhaps even critically) read *Fifty Shades of Grey* are the same: passionate adventurers who yearn for the unknown and the forbidden.

We are Love seekers demanding more from life—not necessarily more stuff, but more intimacy, connection, mystery, awe—and sex. Not the thirty-second-sneeze type, but the unadulterated, long-lasting "Ravish me!" kind that leaves us looking deep into the eyes of our beloved for an hour and, seeing only the Divine there, declaring, "I would do anything for you... anything."

So how do we go from being adventurous, spiritual, wanton wannabes to red-hot and holy? It's simple. The secret is to willingly and shamelessly surrender to our partner.

How? you ask.

Play the Yin Yang game.

In Eastern philosophy, Yin and Yang are complementary forces. Yin is the valley: slow, soft, passive, wet, dark, and often thought of as feminine. Yang is the mountain: fast, hard, penetrating, sunny, and often thought of as masculine. When perfect Yin meets perfect Yang, something more significant than the parts—a mutual whole—is created. Yin and Yang transform each other, gradually trading places with each other. Everyone has both Yin and Yang aspects.

My husband and I discovered during our journey through the sacred and the profane that the Yin Yang game is a doorway into a whole other level of intimacy. It encouraged us to let go of control and invite a spirit of willingness to rule for a spell. This move, in turn, allowed us to surrender—a precursor to liberation, which provided an opening for profound intimacy.

What exactly is this Yin Yang game?

Well, I could have called it the Master and Servant game, but then I might have lost half my audience, who felt sure that some ritual S & M was not for them. But hang on. Hear me out.

The Yin Yang game is a sacred tool, offering you, for a limited time, the possibility to open entirely to one another without preset boundaries, without conditions, with only acceptance and humble submission.

The practice:

- You and your partner each take a turn for an agreed-upon amount of time—say one or two hours—practicing *perfect surrender* as the Yin (Servant) to the other's loving dominance as the Yang (Master).
- Set up a sacred space (see Chapter 10) to add some reverence to the game and to be sure each partner feels safe and protected.
- During the allotted period, the rule is the Yang partner can ask for *anything,* and the Yin partner complies without argument.
- If, by chance, the Yang partner asks for something the Yin partner truly feels is outside their ability or comfort zone to deliver, the appropriate response is: "Please, Master, I am so sorry, I am unable to comply with your wishes. Is there anything else I can do for you?"
- The Yin partner adopts a kind of "My partner is a God/dess right now and I am humble before him/her" attitude, while the Yang party acts boldly to communicate what they want. (The result is that the couple is likely to explore uncharted territory.)
- You can play the Yin Yang game back-to-back on the same day, each taking a turn at role-playing, but it can be even more fun to split the times up so that each party truly

gets their partner's undivided attention. One day you are unequivocally Yin and on another Yang. You will learn something about yourself and your partner either way.

- Play the game with a light heart and an air of reverence.

Notes: _____

_____
_____
_____
_____
_____
_____
_____

While it might seem that surrendering unequivocally to another's wishes might be the most challenging part of this game, it can also be challenging to be the Yang partner, for you must be vulnerable enough to communicate what you want fearlessly. You must also be prepared to receive the enormous Love that surrender offers.

Bowing before one another, each, in turn, we allow ourselves the possibility of seeing our partner in divine light, no matter what.

We agree to let go of our conditioned responses and judgments and offer them only acceptance and compliance. We see that we are here to serve, and who better to serve than our beloved partner?

So—are you ready to go on a spiritual quest to new and exotic lands? Are you prepared to meet your Master taking the form of your mortal partner?

If so, you will discover what Rumi has said is the secret of the happiest couple he knew:

That once every day for an hour they would treat each other as if they were gods, and would do anything, anything their beloved asked.

— *Their Secret Was* by Rumi (translated by Daniel Ladinsky)

Chapter 12

Staying in Touch with Each Other

If you want to feel transported, you have to take risks. I'm not talking about danger; I'm talking about vulnerability of exposure and exploration that heightens trust.
Deep eroticism is intimate; deep intimacy is erotic.
—Esther Perel

Here we are at the end of a journey to getting naked in the now. We've covered a lot of territories. In this penultimate chapter, we will dive deeper to bridge psychological and physical intimacy, touching and being with one another in the spirit of holy intimacy.

Like a cookbook that introduces you to a whole new cuisine and then helps you plan a menu, I will offer a sample *Naked in the Now* date-day retreat at the end of this chapter. This date-day retreat is an ample opportunity to step outside our usual way of thinking and acting to enter a new state. It means intentionally letting go of what we think we know about ourselves and our partners and discovering each other anew.

In the last chapter, we explored new ways to play together as adults, whether friends or lovers. In this chapter, we will focus on cultivating physical and emotional intimacy with a beloved partner, but don't despair if you do not have a partner! On my journey, many of the most important transformations have happened while I was spending time alone. In fact, every time I go on a group silent retreat, one of the days is designated "solo day." Cheri Huber calls solo day "Holy Leisure Day." I love that. Holy Leisure Day is a day when I am totally silent (of course, no electronic devices either). I spend the day practicing all the different awareness exercises intermingling them with walks outside, writing, and coloring. Skip to the final chapter, Chapter 13, for more on creating your own Holy Leisure Day.

Now, back to our focus here: staying in touch with each other. Before getting to our date-day menu, let's consider what it means to prioritize touching each other. Why is it helpful for our growth? How might it help us get naked in the now?

In my book, staying in touch with each other means

- committing to connect physically (aka *Doing it. Every day.*),
- redefining intimacy to include sweet romance but also crass vulgarity (aka *Afternoon Delight*), and
- allowing sexuality to be a portal to presence (*Stillness at the Heart of Sacred Sex*).

Let's look at these one at a time.

Doing it. Every day.

I bet you think I am talking about sex, right?

Well, I am, but maybe not in the way you think.

I've been married since 1984. And yes, when my husband and I first met, I am sure we "did it" every day, being the passionately *in-love* couple that we were. But over the years we settled into a regular but less frequent schedule, at first making sure that all the proper ingredients were present before doing it: romantic leanings, space, time, energy, feeling close, and mutual juiciness—and later, realizing those things could be hard to come by all at once. So instead, we scheduled it for at least a couple of days a week, which seemed much less romantic, but at least helped us commit *some* time and focus on one another to foster intimacy. Plus, as we were getting older, the new, less frequent, planned schedule allowed us some time to recover.

A few years ago, however, we upped the ante.

With our awareness practice, we learned over the years that magic happens when you commit to doing something every day—if only for a short period. We called it "making it to the cushion" (as in meditation cushion). In turn, we saw the impact of awareness practice on our lives: breaking conditioned responses, helping heal from trauma, finding some distance from the habitual conversation in the head that continually judges and analyzes, and perpetually scanning for something wrong that needs fixing.

We discovered awareness practice is mental hygiene and, like, oral hygiene, is deserving of our attention every day. Still, it was ridiculously tempting to get talked out of it because we were tired, didn't have time, or didn't feel like it. (Can you imagine not brushing your teeth every day?)

So endeavoring to develop a daily habit, we set out to make it to the cushion every day for at least five minutes. Sitting still for five minutes a day (the mind was sure to remind us) will not likely bring about any earth-shaking results, except it did. What happened is we signaled our commitment. Awareness practice was essential to us.

We wondered if the same was true for experiencing physical intimacy. What if we connected, in bed, every day? Even if just for a short while. What if we did not approach "doing it" as a goal-oriented activity but rather as a daily habit we wanted to cultivate—a chance to be with one another, to appreciate the opportunity to soul-gaze, to pleasure one another without the impulse to bring it to fruition? We knew that the fruition part, at our age, resulted in less energy afterward and a waning of juiciness toward one another.

It seemed so unlikely that this was possible. *Who did we think we were? Twenty-year-olds?* But it was possible, and the subsequent months brought us deeper intimacy than I imagined. We both appreciated the mutual commitment required to engage with one another intimately every day—not to mention agreeing to sublimate the desire to orgasm in favor of simply connecting.

The truth is, the things that I "do" every day reflect my priorities—but often, the day's activities are the product of unconscious conditioned behavior rather than intentional choices reflecting deeper heartfelt priorities.

Once I paid attention to this, my day opened differently. What am I doing every day? How can I signal the intent for my daily activities to match my deepest longing and to contribute to my health and well-being? If I long to be more intimate with my partner, can I co-create a time for us to connect? Can I engage in being physical with my partner without it being a goal-oriented focus for release?

We began building a few habits into our day. Now, every morning includes coffee together in bed, an extended juicy naked hug, and a bowing to the other, "I honor you as myself." Many afternoons we reconvene, playing light-hearted physical flirty games with each other, if only for a quarter of an hour. And periodically, but regularly, we schedule an entire date-day or date-afternoon. No other distractions. No electronic devices.

Over the years, we've realized that we approach intimacy differently. I lean toward flowery romance, he toward the vulgar and crass. I lean toward emotional intimacy, he toward physical. But we share the desire to connect. And both approaches are valid—together, they create harmony.

Afternoon Delight

In the poem "Otherwise," Jane Kenyon, former poet laureate of New Hampshire, writes with simplicity and grace about her day and how she appreciates each moment. I particularly like the line in that poem:

At noon I lay down with my mate. It might have been otherwise.

Her way of describing making love with her husband feels dreamy and poetic to me and speaks of seizing the moment. Plus, the reference to sex at noon reminds me of that happy seventies song by the Starland Vocal Band, "Afternoon Delight."

I was surprised when I read an article by her husband, US poet laureate Donald Hall, a *New Yorker* article called "Between Solitude and Loneliness." In the article, Hall describes the same ritual his wife tells, but much more bluntly. He says:

Afterward, we took a twenty-minute nap, gathering energy for the rest of the day, and woke to our daily fuck.

Hearing these two wildly different descriptions of the same ritual (both by poet laureates), I initially thought that Jane's perspective seemed spiritual and poetic, while Donald's seemed pornographic and crass.

But deep down, I knew better.

True, there was a time when I might have judged the word "fuck" as belonging in a non-spiritual bucket (where was the reverence after all?), but my practice has shown me differently. Likewise, there might have been a time when I loathed the idea of just "laying down in the afternoon" (where is the juicy in that?).

But taken together, the words of Jane Kenyon and Donald Hall point to something essential but ineffable I have discovered in my own life, something both spiritual and crass, tender and juicy—a harmonizing of opposites that creates magic. This sexual magic transcends the bounds of ordinary sex, bringing us to an intimacy that may be reverent, still, and otherworldly, but is (let's face it) driven by the concrete act of fucking, in all its delightfully vulgar and achingly sweet forms.

This synthesis of the two perspectives described by these poets—the gentle "laying down in the afternoon" and more coarse "daily fuck"—is our version of "Afternoon Delight."

This daily engagement is born from a mutual spiritual desire to connect deeply, even ethereally, with one another, yet bound to the demands of the physical bodies that fuel it.

The most base and primal instincts of sex—the kissing, licking, sucking, blow-by-blow exploration of each other's bodies—are powerful sensual tools for spiritual practice.

In traditional sitting meditation, we bring our attention repeatedly to our object of concentration: our breath, our mantra, or our senses. We draw attention away from the thinking mind, which lives in the past or future, and encourages us to be attentive to right now.

In sex, drawing back to the senses happens naturally, allowing thoughts to slip easily into the background. Sex is a riveting portal to the present, where intimacy with the moment and each other lives.

I have found our "afternoon delight" to be the most sublime meditation. During it, we serve as each other's object of meditation, cultivating an undistracted mind while playfully holding one another's attention (the poetic) right along with each other's genitals (the crass), thereby harnessing the power of the senses to bring us present.

The atmosphere of our afternoon-delight sessions tends to be playful and light-hearted, as the song of the same name implies, and the intent is clear: we are there to love and be loved, to care for and be taken care of, to be awash with unconditional love. We accept each other exactly as we are: tender and caring as well as dirty and foul-mouthed. My yin and his yang meet.

The juxtaposition of both perspectives—the shadow versus light; the yielding versus penetrating, the master versus slave, the "at noon I lay down with my mate" versus "woke to our daily fuck"—helps us see the yin/yang spiritual whole that happens when opposites harmonize. One cannot exist without the other. And instead of lamenting those differences, we take sanctuary in and delight with one another.

A merging happens as we move through physical sensations while holding each other's gaze. So, naturally, we cultivate the desire to prolong the experience. (Love and Ecstasy, aka "Tantra" training, helps.)

We see that sex has so much more to offer than an avenue for quick release. As we let go of the desire to give in to full orgasm and settle into a long and shared moment, we merge into an ecstatic expression that is irregular and intense but also unified and harmonious, like an improvised song or dance with different cadences and moods. Our engagement is dreamy and poetic but also coarse and penetrating. It is both spiritual and pornographic.

Our afternoon delight is a rhapsody of intimacy.

When this happens, sex becomes sacred—a beautiful portal to shared presence. There is a sense of "mystical union" and profound stillness at the heart of sacred sex.

Stillness at the heart of sacred sex

I've been an awareness practitioner for over twenty-five years now. In that time, I've tried many different kinds and styles of sitting. I've meditated with eyes open and eyes closed, laying down and sitting up. I've practiced counting meditation and mantra meditation; zazen while sitting in an empty room looking at a blank wall and spacious awareness in the Sierra Nevada Mountains with Mt. Whitney behind me and Death Valley before me.

I've learned that meditating is not about chasing my thoughts away. Instead, it's about training the mind to focus—noticing when I've gotten swept away in thoughts and gently returning my focus to the object of meditation: my breath, counting, a mantra, or whatever I have chosen as my focal point.

Because when I do, something magical happens. The room simultaneously quiets and buzzes with energy. The air thickens. Stillness is palpable. I am enlivened and present.

I first learned to meditate at a SkyDancing Tantra™ retreat. I didn't know what to make of it then; I was there for increased intimacy and possibly increased sexual prowess. What did meditation have to do with that?

Our teacher told us meditation provides clarity and that by quieting the mind, meditation allows freshness and innocence to return to the act of lovemaking.

I was to discover it was much more powerful than even that. When one's partner essentially becomes the meditation object, when the act of sex is entered into deliberately, patiently, when, while soul gazing, the focus is returned again and again to the other and the shared space, a remarkable stillness experienced during deep meditation happens. And it can be a shared experience.

Wow.

Today, sacred sexuality is my favorite form of meditation amidst a busy life. It's an engaging activity that boldly draws awareness to bodily sensations happening right now instead of thought. Holding the gaze of another also trains attention away from thinking and back to this moment — as in meditation. Sacred sexuality is a natural playground for the mind to take a break — a portal to stillness. And, prolonging that experience beyond a ten-second release is profoundly enlivening.

In a *Scientific American* article called "The Neurobiology of Bliss — Sacred and Profane"[iii] by Nadia Webb, the author notes that bliss has certain qualities, including a diminution of self-awareness, altered bodily perceptions, and a decrease in pain. Furthermore, she says certain things exacerbate our experience of bliss, while others enhance it.

Chief among the exacerbators is the running critique-organizing conscious experience — a default mechanism of the cognitive mind. In other words, it is the ongoing background stories and running commentary we constantly tell ourselves — the harsh judgments, the not-so-helpful critiques, the endless comparisons. My teacher Joel Morwood calls this the "Story of I" and says that being caught up in the Story of I causes us distress. I have heard another teacher put it this way: we are wired to suffer.

Escaping that continual critical self-observation is bliss. Remember, at the start of this book that I said this is a "no-self, self-help" book? That's what I was pointing to—that getting out of our perpetual self-oriented way of thinking and perceiving the world allows us to relax in the moment—to get present. Of course, we may try to blunt our endless self-analysis with drugs, alcohol, and escapist entertainment. Or, if lucky, we've stumbled upon meditation—one of the few tools proven to offer durable relief reliably.

We also overcome it during sex.

When we experience bliss, we alter our everyday perceptions, reinforcing the experience of unity instead of separateness. Both sex and meditation dissolve the sense of physical boundaries, albeit differently. Meditation changes bodily self-awareness by enhancing activity in specific brain regions (see article mentioned above). Sex does it through a heightened sense of being in one's body, of diving into sensory awareness. Pleasure is another marker of bliss.

In sacred sexuality, we combine the two.

By soul-gazing, our partner becomes the object of our meditation, helping us focus our attention just as we do during regular meditation. Returning to a focal point allows us to disidentify with the running critique typically organizing our experience. At the same time, during sex, we also bring heightened awareness to bodily sensations, which ironically leads to a dissolving of the boundaries of our body and results in an increase in pleasure. The experience is riveting, and we are more willing to embrace and stay with the present moment, less inclined to go off on thought.

If you stay with the practice instead of reaching for release— the moment expands and is marked with a profound, charged stillness. Your lover's eyes will reflect that stillness—and they will see it in you.

Behold mystical union.

My encouragement: try it for yourself. Enliven your lovemaking. See what happens when you practice sex as if it were a meditation. You will be so glad you did.

Below, I've put together a date-day retreat menu for lovers! Sometimes we need to reboot alone and sometimes together. If you are seeking something different from the usual dinner- and-movie date night with your lover, try crafting a *Naked in the Now* date experience! Remember, some of the activities are done one at a time, with one partner being the receiver and one partner being the giver. You will want to allow ample time for each partner to have a chance at each role, or schedule two date days.

Practice #33—Menu for a Date-Day Retreat

Schedule your Date-Day Retreat

To start, intentionally schedule a time to play together in this way. (*Remember the pre-communication stage from Practice #21?*) You will want your time to be undistracted, with no child-care duties or interruptions. Turn all electronic devices off. Schedule as much or as little time as you like, but prepare for at least three to four hours.

Advance Preparation

You will need some preparation, as indicated below. Take a moment to revisit each of the practices listed below to familiarize yourself with the details and flow. Note that the sensory awakening ritual has special preparation requirements.

Setting up a Sacred Space (Practice #25)

Think of this as you might think of getting ready for a dinner party. We want to set the stage for an experience. Pick a room or rooms where your different activities might be located and add some accouterments to make it feel special: flowers, music, incense, candles, or beautiful fabric draped enticingly. It could include an altar with objects that are meaningful to the two of you—things that remind you of good times and play. We want to create the illusion of going on an exotic adventure together. It doesn't need to take much to change the mood of a room. *Revisit Practice #25.*

Sensory Awakening Ritual (Practice #30)

A fun-loving way to start a juicy date-day retreat is with a sensory awakening ritual. This ritual puts us right into our senses, which naturally takes us away from our habitual thinking mind and allows us to be in tune with the moment. Plus, it is frivolous and unusual, bringing in an air of playfulness. The preparation needed beforehand is part of the fun! Decide who will be Giver and who will be the Receiver this round. (Best to swap on another day.) What you will need:

- a blindfold, and
- secret samples for each of the senses: sound, smell, touch, taste, sight.

Revisit Practice #30 to understand the flow, but be prepared to spend an hour or so whisking your partner into a sensual delight while you enliven their senses, one at a time. Then, consider ending the ritual with "sight." When you remove your partner's blindfold, you can sit directly in front of them, ready to engage in the following activity: soul-gazing.

After the ritual, give feedback. Again, this is the perfect time to practice sharing. As the Giver, you might ask questions such as "Which sense did you like best? Did any surprise you?" As the Receiver, you will want to share your experience, but you can also ask the Giver questions, such as "What part was the most fun for you to prepare?" Remember, when not talking, you will be practicing attentive, reflective listening—saying back what you heard.

Soul-Gazing (Practice #23)

When the sensory awakening ritual is over, you will already feel more light-hearted and in tune with each other. Therefore, this is a sweet time to practice soul-gazing (Practice #23).

Begin facing each other, kneeling in front of each other, or sitting on chairs. Follow the guidelines for Practice #23: Soul-Gazing. End with a Heart Salutation and the words "I honor you as an aspect of myself."

Remember to take a moment to share. Allow each of you to speak without interruption while the other only listens.

The feedback time is not a time for conversation so much as a time to witness another person sharing. You can show your attentiveness by repeating back what you heard.

Venus Kriya (Practice #31)

After a bit of soul-gazing, extending it by engaging in a Venus Kriya can be powerful. Sit up straight and continue or return to soul gazing. Bring palms to meet your partners and begin doing Breath of Fire together for two to three minutes. (See Appendix A for instructions on Breath of Fire.) Or until one party indicates they need a break by breathing in sharply and audibly. Remember to share feedback afterward.

Yin Yang game (Practice #32)

After playfully spending an afternoon engaging in a sensory ritual and then connecting deeply through soul-gazing and a Venus Kriya, it can be wonderful to retire to the bedroom for a daring game of Yin Yang. Again, you will have to select one party to be Yin (servant) and one party to be Yang (master). On another day, you will swap these roles. Review the juicy details of Practice #32 so that you know what you are playing together. As Yin party, be prepared to serve your Yang partner in humble devotion *exactly* as they request.

Notes: _____

_____

_____

_____

_____

_____

_____

_____

Chapter 13

Holy Leisure Day

Leisure is only possible when we are at one with ourselves. We tend to overwork as a means of self-escape, as a way of trying to justify our existence.
  —Josef Pieper, *Leisure: The Basis of Culture*

It is 7:30 a.m. on the solo day of the retreat—a day described as set aside for "holy leisure." There will be no formal teachings or sittings, and we will be silent the whole day. Part of me feels nervous about being in charge of the day. What will I do for all that time alone? No listening to the teacher, no asking questions.

Although there is no formal agenda, our teachers encourage us to have a minimal structure in place. I think about how much my kids benefitted from a loose schedule, something marking mealtimes, nap times, and play times.

I look at the bare-bones plan for the solo day.

- Silent group meditation 6:30–7:00
- Breakfast at 7
- Lunch at 12
- Dinner at 6

We are required to sign up for one chore. I sign up to do dishes after dinner. We are encouraged to pick a few times during the day to sit quietly for twenty-four minutes, practicing a technique or two that we learned during the week, and walking slowly for five minutes between sessions. Besides that, we can walk, write in our journals, and nap.

I fill in the schedule a little, deciding I will take a leisurely shower after breakfast and then do three back-to-back sitting times after lunch. During these sitting sessions, I plan to work on Tonglen (Practice #17)—taking suffering into the deepest space of my heart and transmuting it there. I know this will push my limits a little—sitting without the peer pressure of others or a teacher present, but I am curious and mentally commit to it. *For one hour and a half of my life, I can do this*, I think. I will go for a long walk sometime after sitting. Other than that, I am not sure—a long morning and evening await. At home on a day off, any extra time would be filled with chores, chatting, and possibly reading or watching TV. So how will I spend this time?

I wonder about the term "Holy Leisure." It pings something deep inside—a stirring. I explore the concept a little to discover what it means to me. I gather up colored pens and my journal to draw and write outside.

I wander outside with my journal and sit quietly in the grass. As I sit bearing little to no agenda for the day, I begin to feel inside something akin to holy leisure—something similar to what I experienced as a child on summer break.

I am relaxed. I am simply sitting, simply looking. Yet, underneath the panic of "not doing anything," something else simmers.

I look around at the same setting I've seen all week. Then, I pick up my pen to find a poem pouring out from my heart; such is the wonder I feel.

I write:

Sitting in reverence
I see
Life itself,
As the cathedral.

I bow in humble submission,
Bending knee,
Awed by the grandeur,
The immense abundance
And profound stillness everywhere.

I am overcome with gratitude and appreciation.

Life's arms envelop me
In warmth,
So that my small self
lets down its ever-present guard.
Those arms of gratitude
make me feel
safe and loved.

Presence steps in, and the heart cries:

THIS is what I want... delight irreverently escapes the last boundary

There is no "I."
only wonder,
innocence,
play.

Holy Leisure Day is an opportunity to relax truly—not watching-a-good-movie type of relaxing, but something else. It is an opportunity to deliberately push our "being alone without distraction" comfort zone. Though it's hard to admit, I have feared that kind of open-ended alone time. It sounds daunting.

What helped me turn the corner was a shift in attitude from a trepid "I have nothing to do" perspective to a curious "What might holy leisure feel like to me?" That, combined with a tiny bit of structure and a commitment to practice while innocently exploring my surroundings, brought me to the poetic escape I describe above—a pure moment of delight in being—naked in the now—no "I," no "other." Present.

Below, I have sketched out a sample Holy Leisure Day schedule so you get the idea. Feel free to re-craft it in a way that feels resonant to you.

Practice #34—Menu for a Holy Leisure Day

Schedule your Holy Leisure Day retreat

To start, intentionally schedule a day or part of a day to set aside for this experiment. You will want your time to be undistracted, with no child-care duties or interruptions. Turn all electronic devices off. Schedule as much or as little time as you like, but prepare for at least three to four hours.

Advance Preparation

Create a menu for yourself to support yourself with proper nourishment. Food preparation can be done as its own Holy Leisure Day activity, but be sure you have all ingredients on hand. Look up a simple series of stretches to do. Have a journal ready for the day and possibly some coloring, painting tools, or a camera. It can be very enlivening to pay attention to one's surroundings by writing about them, drawing them, or taking creative photographs. (If you use your phone as a camera, commit to *not* using it as a phone or internet device.) Have a timer accessible.

Create a schedule (example schedule below)

The idea is to create a scaffolding that encourages some quiet time, some physically active time, some time in nature (or otherwise immersed in your senses), some light play, and some time for gentle introspection. Having a schedule makes it easier to commit to the day. Move slowly between sessions. No rush.

- 7:00 a.m.—Breakfast prep, eating, and cleanup. Dress for the day.
- Clean up afterward. Permit yourself to enjoy the chore of cleaning up.

- 8:00 a.m. — Yoga or light stretches.
- Wake the body up by gently stretching it.
- 8:30 a.m. — Intentional awareness and embodiment practice. (Practices #1 and #3)
- Plan to do several back-to-back sessions of fifteen to twenty minutes with a five-minute break to walk, stretch, and use the restroom. The idea here is to gently practice relaxing the body, drawing attention from the thinking mind to the whole experience of embodiment, pushing your boundaries a little, and sitting longer than you might otherwise. (This is also a good time to experiment with the Pranayama exercises in Appendix A.)
- 10:00 a.m. — Go outside with your journal, allow words to flow. (Practice #5)
- Spend time in nature. Find a place to sit for a short while. Hone your witnessing skills. When ready, set a ten-minute timer and free-write to this prompt: *Right now, I notice...* Free-write to other prompts, such as *I feel...*, *I love...,* or *I see...*
- 11:00 a.m. — Letting guidance in. (Practice #12)
- If you have tarot cards or *I Ching* tokens, this is a perfect opportunity to get quiet inside and listen for any burning questions you have about your life. Once you have formulated your question, sit quietly and do a reading. Take notes.
- Letting go of who you think you are. (Practices #14 and #15)
- If consulting divination cards is not your thing, practice shaking up your conditioned beliefs about who or what you are. Try Bone Breathing (Practice #14) or Naked Awareness (Practice #15). Take notes.
- Noon — Lunch preparation, eating, and cleanup.
- 1:00 p.m. — Go for a long walk; practice recording and listening. (Practice #7)

- Take a recording device with you to record and listen to yourself, talking kindly to yourself—consider speaking out loud a love letter to yourself. (Practice #7)
- 2:00 p.m.—Take a long shower or bath or allow yourself to rest or nap.
- 2:30 p.m.—Heal relationships with others. (Practice #16, 17, or 18)
- Spend the afternoon practicing techniques that help restore and rejuvenate your relationship with others. Choose which practice or practices call to you.
- Heal your relationship with yourself. (Practices 17, 24)
- Acknowledge the importance of treating yourself well. Practice a technique that encourages you to accept yourself and believe in your ability to transmute any suffering.
- 4:30 p.m.—Dinner preparation
- 5:00 p.m.—Dinner

Notes: _____

_____
_____
_____
_____
_____
_____
_____
_____
_____
_____

Appendix A:
Pranayama—Controlled Breathing Exercises

The following are very useful intentional breathing exercises known as Pranayama. If you don't know what to do to stabilize your attention you can always resort to practicing this simple breathwork. These exercises have been used for centuries by meditation teachers from around the world in all traditions. Today, they are used regularly by physicians, therapists, yoga instructors, Zen masters, and mindfulness teachers. A recent popular self-help book *Breath: The New Science of a Lost Art* by James Nestor closely examines ancient breathing practices and explores the hidden science behind them. I highly recommend his book.

Alternate nostril breathing

Alternate nostril breathing can help balance our nervous system, calm our mind, and improve our stress response. It can slow the heartbeat and lower blood pressure. It is one of the oldest Hatha Yoga practices, dating back thousands of years. Some say it is the most powerful breathing practice known in yoga.

Use your thumb to block off one nostril; breathe in.

At the top of the breath, block the other nostril with your index or middle finger, and breathe out.

Then, keeping the same nostril blocked, breathe in.

At the top of the next breath, switch to block off the other nostril and breathe out.

The rhythm if you start by blocking your right nostril would be: in through the left, switch, out through the right; in through the right, switch, out through the left.

Repeat for eight or nine cycles.

4-7-8 breathing

This technique is sometimes called the "relaxing breath." Dr. Andrew Weil teaches this technique because he believes it reduces anxiety, helps promote sleep, manages cravings, and controls or reduces anger. It is part of one of the exercises in this book, Tonglen (Practice #17).

Inhale for a count of 4.

Hold the breath for a count of 7.

Exhale strongly for a count of 8.

Repeat for 4 cycles.

Double the exhale (aka Zen breathing)

We have recently begun participating with the Las Vegas Zen Center. Zen Master Ji Haeng regularly reminds us to inhale naturally and deeply into our abdomen and build a practice of long, slow exhalations. Our goal is that the exhalation be twice as long as the inhalation. This practice, which is as old as the Buddha, is recognized in modern parlance as helping us hack our vagus nerve, improving our heart-rate variability, counteracting fight-or-flight mode, and improving decision-making.

Breathe naturally into the abdomen. (You can count how long your natural breath is.)

Exhale long and slow for twice the length of the inhale.

Repeat for as long as you like. (Even two minutes is said to be beneficial.)

Breath of Fire (aka fast Pranayama)

Breath of fire is a common component of Kundalini yoga, and has been cited with similar benefits to other breathing exercises. In addition, it helps strengthen your diaphragm and helps your lungs take in more air. It is part of one of my favorite partner exercises, called a Venus Kriya (Practice #31).

Start in a seated position, either cross-legged or in a chair.

Place your hand face up in your lap (unless instructed to use another position).

Inhale through your nose, allowing your belly to expand.

Without pausing, forcefully exhale through the nose while contracting (pulling in) your abdominal muscles.

Continue the rhythm of inhaling passively and exhaling forcefully. Focus in on the exhale. You can increase your speed as you go.

Repeat for up to thirty seconds or as long as three minutes.

Circular breathing (aka rebirthing)

Circular breathing is practiced by some musicians to produce a continuous tone without interruption. It is also part of a practice known as Rebirthing breathwork or Conscious Connected breathwork. A similar practice is called Holotropic breathwork. In circular breathing there is no pause between the inhale and the exhale; instead, the breath is continuous. This kind of breathing can put you in a kind of altered state of consciousness. You might revisit trauma and release energy blockages or expose unconscious defense mechanisms. This kind of breathwork is best undertaken with a guide. Once during a rebirthing class, I had a powerful vision where I was visited by an old man who had wisdom to share with me. Another time, I found myself crying buckets of tears.

Appendix B:
Tarot Reading for *Naked in the Now:*
Juicy Practices for Getting Present

I was working with the Osho Zen Tarot card deck. The first card pulled holding the position of the "central issue" was Major Arcana card number 1:

I Existence.

The picture shows a naked woman sitting on the lotus leaf of perfection, knowing that "home" is a place of inner relaxation and acceptance. If there was one single card in the entire deck that might encapsulate the subject matter of this book, this card is it. It is one of only two cards in the deck of 79 cards depicting a naked person; both cards appeared in this reading.

In the second position, to the left, representing "internal influence you are unable to see," appeared another Major Arcana card, number XIX:

XIX Beyond Illusion.

The card depicts the face of consciousness overlayed on a butterfly. It is a card that reminds us not to look at the surface but to look within — to go beyond our judgments.

In the third position, to the right of the central issue, standing for the "external influence of which you are aware," appeared the other card depicting a naked person:

Queen of Water (Receptivity).

The picture shows a naked and headless woman with arms reaching up. She has no head, so her aggressive mind does not hinder her pure receptivity. She reminds us to listen so intently that we forget our habitual self-centered focus.

In the fourth position, below the central issue, standing for "what is needed for resolution," appeared this card:

Five of Clouds (Comparison).

The picture is of a bamboo stalk next to an oak trunk. It's about being yourself and fulfilling your own potential.

The fifth card, above the central issue, in the position of "the resolution," appeared:

Page of Water (Understanding).

The picture is of birds looking out from what looks like a cage, but the cage has no doors, and the bars are disappearing. It is a card about the dawning of a new understanding where we can spread our wings and fly free.

Appendix C:
I Ching Reading for *Naked in the Now: Juicy Practices for Getting Present*

I pulled the following stones in this order:

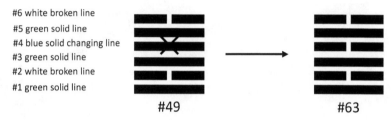

#6 white broken line
#5 green solid line
#4 blue solid changing line
#3 green solid line
#2 white broken line
#1 green solid line

#49 → #63

Picture 3 – Hexagram 49 to 63

The resulting first hexagram is #49. Because the top trigram has a changing line in it, then there will be a second hexagram, which is #63.

The example above my first hexagram, #49, called "Skinning/ Revolution," is all about stripping away the old and letting new life emerge (as in shedding a skin). (Notice how this is similar to the Beyond Illusion card in the tarot reading—one using a snake shedding its skin, the other using the image of a butterfly having transformed from a caterpillar.)

The text for hexagram #49 says it is time to remove a protective layer and indicates this is a positive move and a whole new cycle beginning.

As I read through all the text available, the word "kindness" jumps out at me. I move on to read the interpretive text about changing line in position 4, which reiterates the message saying again to have no doubts and that there is the possibility to transform the imaginative basis of my world.

Finally, I read the text about the hexagram it is changing into, #63, which is called "already fording." The text indicates that the action is already underway. The symbol is in the crossing of a great river and being already halfway across. It says to adapt to whatever crosses my path and to give aid and encouragement, counseling me to stay with the process, but not to hurry to completion, rather remaining underway.

To someone actively writing a book, this reading relaxes me. I am on a good path. I should simply keep moving on, not worry about being done, but rather focusing on aiding and encouraging others as I go.

My preferred *I Ching* book:

I Ching: The Classic Chinese Oracle of Change: The First Complete Translation with Concordance by Stephen Karcher

Endnotes

i. Derived from Natalie Goldberg's practice as described in *Writing Down the Bones: Freeing the Writer Within*, Shambhala; Anniversary edition, 2016

ii. "New Study Finds That Kundalini Yoga Can Help Treat Symptoms of Generalized Anxiety Disorder" by Andrea Rice, August 2020, Yoga Journal.

iii. https://www.scientificamerican.com/article/the-neurobiology-of-bliss-sacred-and-profane/

O-BOOKS

SPIRITUALITY

O is a symbol of the world, of oneness and unity; this eye
represents knowledge and insight. We publish titles on general
spirituality and living a spiritual life. We aim to inform and
help you on your own journey in this life.
If you have enjoyed this book, why not tell other readers
by posting a review on your preferred book site?

Recent bestsellers from O-Books are:

Heart of Tantric Sex
Diana Richardson
Revealing Eastern secrets of deep love and intimacy
to Western couples.
Paperback: 978-1-90381-637-0 ebook: 978-1-84694-637-0

Crystal Prescriptions
The A-Z guide to over 1,200 symptoms and their healing crystals
Judy Hall
The first in the popular series of eight books, this handy little
guide is packed as tight as a pill bottle with crystal remedies
for ailments.
Paperback: 978-1-90504-740-6 ebook: 978-1-84694-629-5

Shine On
David Ditchfield and J S Jones
What if the aftereffects of a near-death experience were
undeniable? What if a person could suddenly produce
high-quality paintings of the afterlife, or if they
acquired the ability to compose classical symphonies?
Meet: David Ditchfield.
Paperback: 978-1-78904-365-5 ebook: 978-1-78904-366-2

The Way of Reiki
The Inner Teachings of Mikao Usui
Frans Stiene
The roadmap for deepening your understanding of the
system of Reiki and rediscovering your
True Self.
Paperback: 978-1-78535-665-0 ebook: 978-1-78535-744-2

You Are Not Your Thoughts.
Frances Trussell
The journey to a mindful way of being, for those who want
to truly know the power of mindfulness.
Paperback: 978-1-78535-816-6 ebook: 978-1-78535-817-3

The Mysteries of the Twelfth Astrological House
Fallen Angels
Carmen Turner-Schott, MSW, LISW
Everyone wants to know more about the most misunderstood
house in astrology — the twelfth astrological house.
Paperback: 978-1-78099-343-0 ebook: 978-1-78099-344-7

WhatsApps from Heaven
Louise Hamlin
An account of a bereavement and the extraordinary
signs — including WhatsApps — that a retired
law lecturer received from her deceased husband.
Paperback: 978-1-78904-947-3 ebook: 978-1-78904-948-0

The Holistic Guide to Your Health
& Wellbeing Today
Oliver Rolfe
A holistic guide to improving your complete health,
both inside and out.
Paperback: 978-1-78535-392-5 ebook: 978-1-78535-393-2

Cool Sex
Diana Richardson and Wendy Doeleman
For deeply satisfying sex, the real secret is to reduce the heat,
to cool down. Discover the empowerment and fulfilment
of sex with loving mindfulness.
Paperback: 978-1-78904-351-8 ebook: 978-1-78904-352-5

Creating Real Happiness A to Z
Stephani Grace
Creating Real Happiness A to Z will help you understand
the truth that you are not your ego
(conditioned self).
Paperback: 978-1-78904-951-0 ebook: 978-1-78904-952-7

A Colourful Dose of Optimism
Jules Standish

It's time for us to look on the bright side, by boosting
our mood and lifting our spirit, both in our interiors,
as well as in our closet.

Paperback: 978-1-78904-927-5 ebook: 978-1-78904-928-2

Readers of ebooks can buy or view any of these bestsellers by
clicking on the live link in the title. Most titles are published
in paperback and as an ebook. Paperbacks are available in
traditional bookshops. Both print and ebook formats are
available online.

Find more titles and sign up to our readers' newsletter at
www.o-books.com

Follow O books on Facebook at **O-books**

For video content, author interviews and more, please subscribe to our YouTube channel:

O-BOOKS Presents

Follow us on social media for book news, promotions and more:

Facebook: O-Books

Instagram: @o_books_mbs

Twitter: @obooks

Tik Tok: @ObooksMBS

www.o-books.com